"A great read!"

I read *Take Up the S*  cally, has great
personal stories, an· ... ·v enforcement
or for people who v ... put on a "uniform" every day.

BILL FAY
Author, former police chaplain

As a law enforcement officer there is a real battle on the streets but
that battle is much deeper than between the good and the bad. It is
a battle that rages in the hearts and minds of our heroes behind the
badge and there are souls in danger if that battle is not won. *Take
Up the Shield* is a necessary tool for victory.

CAPTAIN TRAVIS YATES
Tulsa Police Department
Director, Ten-Four Ministries

An inspirational message, delivered with honesty, humility, and a
sense of humor. In straight talk from a cop's perspective, this mod-
ern look at the believer's armor provides all Christians, not just
peace officers, with a fresh view of faith survival training. As a cop,
I want training to do two things: to make me think and to challenge and equip me to be better. This book accomplishes both.

CAPTAIN CARL DEELEY
Los Angeles County Sheriff's Department

Take Up the Shield is a great read! God has truly gifted Tony Miano
with an ability to draw the reader into his stories and then back it
all up with solid Bible teaching.

DEPUTY BRYAN WHITE
Los Angeles County Sheriff's Department

Fellow officers, *Take Up the Shield* is must reading. Weapons, body
armor, training—these are the things that can save you in this life.
What Tony Miano shares in these pages can save you in the life to
come.

TOM HOLLAND
Detective, FBI Special Agent, Police Chief (Ret.)

Take Up the Shield is outstanding and I look forward to being able to place it into the hands of police officers.

LT. DEVIN CHASE
Torrance Police Department
Board of Directors, Peace Officers for Christ International

It is refreshing to read a book designed to strengthen the Christian walk of the peace officer. *Take Up the Shield* is well written and completely relevant for the challenges facing officers in our society.

CHAPLAIN GARY MALKUS
San Bernardino County Sheriff's Department
Board of Directors, Peace Officers for Christ International

Police officers are members of the "Warrior Class." If, as a police officer, you have ever felt like you're in a constant battle, you should read this book. Tony Miano has used his experience as a working cop and chaplain to identify the physical and spiritual battles officers face. If you or a loved one wear the badge, you'll find this book very helpful in answering the deep, professional and personal questions police officers ask.

HOWARD EDDY
District Attorney Investigator III (Ret.)

This encouraging word is for those who are in and outside of the law enforcement family—as peace officers, soldiers, and all who protect our freedom and liberty face the enemy on a regular basis and need our prayers for protection and strength. I highly recommend this book to all law enforcement or military families as it is relevant to today's defenders of freedom.

SUZANNE RAE DESHCHIDN
Christian Book Previews.com

Tony Miano has a deep love for and a sense of duty toward the law enforcement family. You will enjoy reading this book, and every officer who reads it will immediately identify with its content. This is a book you are going to want to share with others.

PASTOR W. RONALD SEIDEL, SR.
Granada Hills Community Church
Los Angeles Reserve Police Officer and Department Chaplain

TAKE UP
the SHIELD

COMPARING THE UNIFORM OF THE
POLICE OFFICER *&* THE ARMOR OF GOD

TONY MIANO

genesis
PUBLISHING GROUP

Take Up the Shield: Comparing the Uniform of the Police Officer & the Armor of God

Genesis Publishing Group
2002 Skyline Place
Bartlesville, OK 74006
www.genesis-group.net

Cover, design, and production by Genesis Group

Printed in the United States of America

Sixth printing, 2013

ISBN 978-0-9749300-7-7

Unless otherwise indicated, Scripture quotations are from *The New American Standard Bible*, © 1960, 1962, 1963, 1968, 1971, 1972, 1973, 1975, 1977, 1995 by The Lockman Foundation. Used by permission.

CONTENTS

To my loving wife, Mahria,
the best "partner" this street cop
could ever hope to have. Mahria has been a
cop's wife for almost twenty years. The Lord has
powerfully used Mahria as she has supported me
as my counselor, my confidante, my partner in
ministry, my "backup," and my very best friend.
Mahria is a wonderful example to me, and
to others, of the biblical admonition,
"Through love serve one another"
(Galatians 5:13).

ACKNOWLEDGMENTS

I am blessed to have many friends, brothers and sisters in Christ, who have invested in my life and the ministry to which God has called me. Several of these special people have helped me to bring this work from sermon text to book form. I would first like to thank Pastor Jeff Steele, who was my first pastor after I came to faith in Jesus Christ. Jeff encouraged me to use the gift he believed God had given me to write and to teach. Pastor Jeff was my mentor then, and continues to this day to be a good friend.

I would like to thank Pastor Dave DeVries for first suggesting that I speak about the armor of God, using the uniform of the police officer to illustrate each piece of armor. I have been blessed with the opportunity to bring this message a number of times. Pastor Dave was instrumental in helping me to take the step of faith to enter full-time ministry.

My thanks also go to several people who took the time to pore over the various drafts of this book. These friends include my pastor—Pastor Ron Seidel of Granada Hills Community Church (a fellow street cop and chaplain), Pastor Steve Cooley, Chaplain Warren Johnson, Chaplain Neil McAllister, Pastor/Chaplain Gary Malkus, Detective John Howard, Pastor/Chaplain Jack Abeelen, Captain Carl Deeley, Lieutenant Rick Nutt, Lieutenant Devin Chase, Sergeant Mike and Kirsten O'Brien, Deputy/Pastor Bryan White, Jason Cox, Ian Pari, Greg Vonada, and Donna Cook (Mom). Their caring, honest input was very helpful in fine-tuning the direction and flow of the text, as well as in ensuring that

I rightly handle the Word of God. I am also thankful to Mahria, who has patiently and lovingly read just about everything I have written during my Christian life.

I would like to express my appreciation to Scott and Michele Ponder for their prayerful and practical support. They provided great encouragement at a time when it was needed most. And I am grateful for the unknown number of people, inside and outside the law enforcement community, who prayed about the publication of this book.

I would like to thank Lynn Copeland, of Genesis Publishing Group, for believing in this book and for holding my hand through the publishing process. She has taught me much about being a writer and about the literary world. I like associating myself with people who care about my law enforcement family. And I count Lynn among this special group.

My thanks go to Joanne Edgington-Henning for the fine work she did in editing this book. Joanne is a professional writer and the loving wife of a Christian peace officer. Her caring and sacrificial efforts speak to her love for Christ and for the law enforcement family.

And, most important, I would like to thank my Lord and Savior Jesus Christ for the gift of eternal life, and for the privilege of serving Him as my life's work and calling. If there is any glory, praise, and thanks to be given as you read this book, may it be given to Him and Him alone.

ing in law enforcement, I hope the illustrations will give you a better understanding of life behind the badge and the special people who make up the law enforcement community.

You don't have to be a cop or a Christian to be encouraged and challenged by this book. In addition to building your faith, may this book also serve as a helpful introduction to the men and women who protect you and your community.

Chapter One

My First Uniform

They called it the "grinder." When my academy experience began, I had no idea what that meant. I would learn soon enough. Though technically the "grinder" was a place, its significance was not its location as much as it was what happened to an unsuspecting soul (like me) once he or she got there. The "grinder" was a section of the academy parking lot where drill instructors applied the unique skills of their vocation as they ground recruits—like a butcher grinds hamburger out of a chunk of beef—into remnants of their former selves. The goal was to shatter each recruit's self-absorbed sense of individuality in order to mold them collectively into a cohesive unit.

The uniform of the day, and for the first few weeks of training, was business attire (suits). Though already hired by the department, recruits had to earn the right to wear the uniform of a Los Angeles County Deputy Sheriff. That was achieved by successfully completing the various phases of physical, academic, and tactical training—and by surviving the "grinder."

The most dreaded assignment for the recruit was that of class sergeant, who was given the responsibility of marching the class to and from the various locations, calling cadence, and taking roll. This *was not* a coveted position among recruits, at least not during the first several weeks of training. Those selected to be class sergeant early in the academy were not chosen for their natural abilities or military bearing. On the contrary, the class sergeant was often the recruit who caught the predatory eye of one or more of the drill instructors. Deficiencies in performance, bearing, or attitude were some of the indicators that drill instructors looked for in recruits when determining who should be the next class sergeant.

While we felt for Art because of the pain he was about to endure, each of us was thinking, Better you than me, buddy.

If a recruit survived the stint as class sergeant—which could last from a day to a week (or longer)—he or she would be summarily dismissed back to the platoon. The march back to the ranks was often accompanied by the drill instructors' personal critiques, which were often laced with expletives and other insulting jargon. These were the days before the term "political correctness" was on the radar of society's consciousness.

One of the drill instructors would then bark the question we recruits quickly learned to dread: *Who wants to be class sergeant?* Every recruit's right hand would shoot into the air, hoping against hope that his or her name would not be called. Not raising your hand guaranteed your immediate recruitment into the position.

"Who wants to be class sergeant?" one of the drill instructors yelled. My right hand, along with a hundred other right hands, shot skyward. The drill instructor who asked the question called out the name of the unfortunate individual chosen to serve as our next class sergeant. "Recruit Mitchell, get up here!"

Our platoons were organized in alphabetical order. Art Mitchell was in my platoon, and he stood immediately to my right. Art sighed (not loud enough for a drill instructor to hear, however) as he picked up his briefcase (containing our training manuals, which we carried with us at all times) and began to make his way to the front of the class. Relieved, the rest of us put our hands down and stood at attention. Inwardly, every recruit's emotions were mixed. I know mine were. While we felt for Art because of the pain he was about to endure, each of us was thinking, *Better you than me, buddy.*

Art made it about halfway to the front of the class when the air was pierced by the thundering voice of our "Ramrod" (the lead drill instructor), Deputy Johnson. "No! No! No!" he yelled. "I want recruit Miano up here!"

Enthusiastic or Just Stressed Out?

I couldn't believe my ears. The Ramrod had just personally picked me to be the next class sergeant. My mind raced as I tried to figure out what I had done to raise the hackles of the Ramrod. I was ranked in the top half of the class in every discipline, and I tried my best not to draw too much negative attention to myself.

I picked up my briefcase and made my way around the class to the front. I could feel every eye upon me. Some people would have considered this a good time to pray— but the thought never crossed my mind. At that point in my life, as I stood on the hot blacktop, wondering if the health spa where I worked prior to being hired by the Sheriff's Department would take me back, I didn't care about God. As far as I was concerned, God hadn't helped me before, and I wasn't expecting Him to help me now. I figured I was alone, and I could find a way out of the mess in which I found myself. I was wrong.

All the drill instructors were huddled off to one side of the class. I could feel their sinister smiles on the back of my neck as I passed them, being sure not to make even *peripheral* eye contact with them. They were like a school of sharks, and they could smell blood in the water—my blood. I centered myself in front of the class, stood at attention, and waited for my first set of instructions. I was nervous. I was scared. And I didn't have a clue. The only thing I knew about military close-order drill was what I learned from some of my favorite John Wayne movies. Again, let me reiterate, I didn't have a clue.

Deputy Arviso, a short and stocky street cop, a veteran of the streets of East Los Angeles, was the drill instructor who now stood in front of me. After a few excruciating moments of silence, Deputy Arviso spoke. "Recruit Miano," he said, "we don't know if you're overly enthusiastic or just stressed out, but we're going to find out this week."

Overly enthusiastic or stressed out? I thought. *Why do they think I'm stressed out?* I *was* stressed out, but I couldn't figure out what I had done to show it.

Deputy Arviso then very quietly gave me a piece of sage advice that shed some light on why I found myself in such an unenviable position. He said, "When an instructor addresses you, it is not necessary for you to yell your response at the top of your lungs." I immediately knew what he was talking about. With Hollywood providing my only "military training," I thought that any time someone in authority spoke to me, I should respond very firmly—and even louder still. So, that's exactly what I did. Although I looked at my actions as a show of commitment and enthusiasm, I could certainly see why someone on the receiving end of my enthusiasm might mistake it for stress. The truth is, I did use my enthusiasm to mask my stress, or so I thought.

Deputy Arviso stepped away, beyond the range of my peripheral vision, only to be quickly replaced by the Ramrod, Deputy Johnson. "Recruit Miano," he began, "do you have any military experience?"

He knew full well that I didn't have any military experience. Every recruit was required to write a short autobiography prior to the start of the academy. I couldn't lie. That would have been a breach of integrity and the end of my career, before it ever got started. But simply saying "no" wasn't an option either. That was the answer he wanted, and it would have given him one more reason (not that he needed one) to read me the riot act.

Looking straight ahead, without making eye contact with the Ramrod, I said the first thing that came to mind. This is a manner of response—both before that particular day and since—that has not always brought me the desired positive reaction from the person with whom I'm speaking.

"Sir, no, sir!" I yelled. "But I was a high-ranking Webelos Scout!"

"My Life is Over!"

I couldn't believe what had just come out of my mouth. For those of you unfamiliar with the rank structure of the Cub Scouts of America, a Webelos Scout is the highest Cub Scout rank before a youngster enters the Boy Scouts. Recalling the achievement of my youth, and doing so loud enough for every recruit and instructor to hear, had a noticeable impact on all who were present. It was not the impact I had hoped for, but certainly the kind I should have expected—had I been thinking.

As soon as the words left my mouth, the Ramrod's cheeks filled with air, in an obvious attempt to keep from laughing and losing his military bearing. He quickly turned and marched to where the rest of the instructors were gathered. I could hear the sharks laughing. And then I noticed the demeanor of the entire class of recruits. My classmates, like the Ramrod, were fighting to keep from breaking into uproarious laughter. They looked like stalks of wheat, swaying back and forth in a swirling breeze, all of them holding their breath until their faces began to turn red.

As I recall that miserable day, all those years ago, I can't help but think of a scene from one of my favorite baseball movies, *The Sandlot*. The movie's main character, Scotty Smalls, heads for the sandlot, hoping to fit in with the other kids by taking up the game of baseball. His hat, which featured a picture of a trout on the front, had a brim that was way too big. His glove was made of plastic. He had a better chance of catching the plague than catching a baseball.

Scotty makes his way through the bushes and finds himself standing in left field, awestruck by the prowess with which the other kids were playing the game. He hears a large dog growl behind him and turns his head just as Benny "The Jet" Rodriguez rips a long fly ball to left field. Scotty hears the other kids yell, "Watch out!" He turns back just in time to see the white, round missile heading straight for his face. Scotty throws his arms in front of his face, screams, and falls to the ground just before the ball glances off his glove.

As to be expected, the other kids laugh at Scotty's miscue. In an attempt to redeem himself, Scotty chases after the ball, which, by now, has rolled into the bushes. He tries to discipline and motivate himself by repeatedly muttering under his breath, "Don't be a goofus!" He picks up the ball after being startled yet again by "the beast"—a very large, junkyard dog. Scotty pulls himself out of the bushes with ball in hand, only to realize that he doesn't know how to throw.

After a few awkward seconds of trying to figure out the mechanics of throwing a ball, Scotty does his best to get the ball back into the infield. The ball travels all of three feet, bouncing on the ground in front of him. The other kids are now on the ground, holding their stomachs, and laughing uncontrollably. Scotty puts his head down and mumbles to himself, "My life is over." Then he turns and runs home.

Scotty Smalls, the goofus, I would like you to meet Tony Miano, the high-ranking Webelos Scout.

Scotty and I shared so much that day. As I made my way to the front of the class, I'm sure I mumbled something like, "Don't be a goofus! Don't be a goofus!" Not yet a Christian, I probably added a few very colorful adjectives here and there. And, after I confessed my position in the Cub Scouts to the Ramrod and saw my peers fighting back the laughter, I, like Scotty Smalls, thought, *My life is over!*

I was completely convinced that I would never wear the uniform of a deputy sheriff. My verbal faux pas surely all but guaranteed my early dismissal from the academy. It was just a matter of time. And what would I tell Mahria? How do you tell your wife and mother of your two-month-old daughter that you just lost your job because you bragged about being a high-ranking Webelos Scout?

My sincere, but ridiculous answer to the Ramrod's question was certainly enough cause to warrant the sharks' relentless verbal and non-verbal persecution. I had provided them with ample ammunition. It was just a matter of time until they buried me in disciplinary research papers, broke me down with extra physical conditioning, and wore me out with psychological harassment. I saw it happen to others, and it was about to happen to me. I was sure of it.

Wearing the Uniform

Much to my surprise, not only did I survive to graduate from the academy, but the drill instructors left me alone the entire week I served as class sergeant. They must have considered what I said to be confident sarcasm. Over the years, it's the only conclusion that I've drawn that makes any sense. The drill instructors were wrong, but I wasn't about to challenge their thinking. So, I'm probably the only self-admitted high-ranking Webelos Scout to graduate from the Los Angeles County Sheriff's Department Academy. If there are others out there, they probably have not admitted it. Smart.

Eventually, those who survived the "grinder" and their stints as class sergeant were allowed to put on the uniform of a deputy sheriff. I remember the first time I ever put mine on, complete with all the necessary equipment. My emotions were mixed. There was certainly a sense of pride, and a sense of accomplishment. There was also a little apprehension. Would I be able to live up to everything the uniform represented? Although I would graduate from the academy, I still had many questions about the extent of my responsibilities to the department, my fellow deputies, and the communities I would serve. And I was pretty clueless about the stigma and animosity that would come from those who had little or no regard, nor any respect, for the uniform and what it represented. I still had much to learn.

And, as good as it felt to be in uniform, it wasn't very comfortable at first. It was cumbersome. It itched. The equipment was heavy. Even though it was a custom fit, it didn't feel natural. What I learned was that I had to grow into my uniform. I had to adjust to the uniform, not the other way around. It didn't take long for the uniform to become comfortable, because I wore it every day. Over time, it became so comfortable, in fact, that it was no more of an encumbrance than a pair of jeans and a T-shirt. And, since 1987, I've probably worn my uniform more than any other suit of clothes in my wardrobe (such as it is).

As I'm sure is the case with most, if not all, members of the law enforcement community, the thought of working regular patrol out of uniform is unacceptable. You don't have to work the streets very long to realize how important each piece of equipment is to your effectiveness, and to your ability to protect yourself and the people you serve. Although newer officers have a tendency to carry more equipment than they probably need—we like to refer to them as "Deputy or Officer Gadget"—it is also true that the "old salts" will sometimes stop carrying necessary equipment for convenience' sake, leaving important pieces of equipment out of their "war bags" and in their lockers.

You don't have to work the streets very long to realize how important each piece of equipment is to your effectiveness.

Wearing the Believer's Uniform

I have been privileged to wear my uniform for many years, and I've come to realize that the various pieces of equipment that I carry, and so often use as I work the streets, make all the difference in my ability to do my job. I've also seen the consequences faced by far too many who either haven't possessed the right equipment, or who have used the right equipment in the wrong way. Moreover, I've come to recognize the similarities between the uniform of the police officer and the believer's armor—the spiritual and practical equipment God gives to those who know Jesus Christ as their Lord and Savior. In Ephesians chapter 6, the apostle Paul lists the armor and explains that it is given for the purpose of serving God and protecting against Satan's attacks. The similarities between the uniform of the police officer and God's armor go beyond the pieces of equipment themselves, however. They extend to the importance of preparation for duty and the cost when we fail to use the right equipment in the right way. We must understand how to "wear" and "use" this armor as God's peace officer, if you will.

The important thing to note here, however, is that it is faith in Jesus Christ that allows an individual to wear the spiritual armor of God. More specifically, it is my faith in Jesus Christ that allows me to be one of God's peace officers. So that is where I will start.

Chapter Two

THE TESTIMONY OF A CHANGED LIFE

I graduated from the academy on September 18, 1987. My first assignment was to the Pitchess Detention Center, a medium-security facility. What a culture shock! I had led a pretty sheltered life up to that point. Nothing in my experience, or during my time in the academy for that matter, could have prepared me for life inside the jail. I quickly learned that the rules there were similar to the animal kingdom. It was survival of the fittest with the strong preying upon the weak.

I worked very hard in the jail to prove myself as a competent deputy. In a month's time, I often made more than twenty felony arrests of inmates for weapons and drug charges. Remember, these are people who are already incarcerated. I was told that there were a couple of months in which I made more arrests than entire shifts at some of the slower patrol stations. I was completely consumed by my work. I lived it. I breathed it. I looked at each day in the jail as my preparation for the day I would work the streets. That was my ultimate goal—to be the best street cop in the department. And the inmates I guarded served as a means to that end. My only concern for them was how they could provide me with my next arrest stat, or what they could tell me about life on the streets.

A sergeant, who had been one of my firearms instructors in the academy, took me under his wing. He soon made me a training officer for newly assigned deputies, so I thought his interest in me was strictly professional. He was considered a "cop's cop" who had "been there, done that," having worked some of the toughest streets in the county. Known for his no-nonsense approach to police work, he had the stories to back it up. He was "old school," and that impressed me. However, the sergeant was concerned with more than just my career path. He was concerned about where I would spend eternity.

Eternity was a subject I hadn't thought much about.

Church—Like It or Not

My early years were spent in one of many small steel-mill towns in western Pennsylvania where the predominant religion was Roman Catholicism. The predominant ethnicity of the area was eastern European (Czech, Polish, etc.). Being of Italian extraction, my family attended the Roman Catholic church downtown with other Italians, instead of one of the several parishes that dotted the hillsides surrounding our home.

I dreaded going to church, especially catechism classes. The nuns were unfriendly. The priests were intimidating and unapproachable, and they often spoke in a language I didn't understand. Sunday, as far as I was concerned, was a day God created so that kids like me could play baseball. In fact, the other six days of the week were made for the same activity. As James Earl Jones said, while playing the role of a blind former Negro League baseball great in *The Sandlot*, "Baseball was life. And I was good at it." But as an Italian kid growing up in western Pennsylvania, you went to church, like it or not.

I grew up believing what I had been taught: that Jesus was the Son of God, that He came to earth and was born of a virgin, that He died on the cross, and that He rose from the dead. But I also grew up believing all Italians went to heaven.

I believed that heaven was a real place. I believed that hell was a real place (which was any place not within walking distance of a baseball field). I believed that if I did more good than bad in my life, when the time came, I would be able to talk God into letting me into heaven. After all, God must be a reasonable guy. But what I thought of God as a "person" soon soured.

First Disillusionment

When I was about nine or ten years old, my younger sister, Cheri, was very ill and missed her first confession. In the Catholic church, confession was an important and necessary step toward receiving her first communion. In order for her to advance with the rest of her catechism class, she needed to go to confession before her first communion. For whatever reason, we were unable to go to St. Michael's (our parish). My mom dressed Cheri in her pretty communion dress and told me to walk her down the hill to a nearby parish so that the priest could hear her first confession.

That was the last thing I wanted to do. The priest at the parish down the hill was a scary guy. For some reason, he didn't approve of my friends and me playing baseball in the vacant lot adjacent to the church. (It probably had something to do with the stained glass windows we broke from time to time with our deep drives to center field.) In any case, the last thing I wanted to do was come face to face with that parish priest.

But, being a young man of courage, I did what I had to do. I took Cheri by the hand and walked her down the hill to the church. That's where my courage stopped. I stood at the bottom of the stairs and told Cheri to walk up and knock on the door of the church. I had knocked on the door and run too many times before to knock on the door and actually wait for someone to answer. "Ding-dong Ditch" was another popular game among the kids in my town.

Cheri made her way up the stairs. The doors looked even bigger with my little sister walking toward them. I told her to hurry up and that I would be waiting for her outside when she was done. Cheri knocked on the door. I hoped against hope that no one would answer. My hopes were dashed when I heard the door creak and I watched, petrified, as it slowly opened.

I couldn't believe what I had just heard. I remember thinking, What kind of God has a guy like that working for Him?

Cheri looked up at the priest who stuck his head out the door. She told him that she was there to have him hear her first confession. He looked at her with no love or compassion in his eyes, and he said, "Go away. Your kind is not welcome here." He closed the door leaving my little sister standing alone at the top of the stairs.

I couldn't believe what I had just heard. I remember thinking, *What kind of God has a guy like that working for Him?* I walked my dejected little sister home. That baseball season, I swung for those stained glass windows with a little more determination. I never wanted to go to church again. As far as I was concerned, God was like that old priest—mean and unapproachable. But, believing He was still God, I tried not to tick Him off too much.

My family soon moved to California. Within a couple of years, my mom and dad divorced. I was beginning to doubt if God had any control whatsoever over what happens on earth. And I was mad at Him. *What did I ever do to Him?* I thought. So I stopped thinking about Him altogether.

Chasing Gods

Instead, I found a new god—sports. After my parents divorced and things were tough at home (and they often were), I escaped into sports. When I was sad or lonely, I found comfort in sports. When I needed encouragement or clarity of mind, I found it in sports. When I needed to hear how good I was, I heard it from those who watched me play sports.

But by the time I turned 15, I no longer found myself at the front of the pack, at the top of the heap of my sports world. Other kids, the *really good* athletes, were passing me by. The recognition I once received was now going to others. My god was turning its back on me, the same way God had turned His back on me so many times (so I believed). So, I gave up on sports, just like I gave up on God.

For the next several years, I tried to fill the void that the absence of sports left in my life with other things and with other people—namely people of the opposite sex. Along the way, I thought about giving God "another shot," but quickly dismissed such ideas as foolishness.

Then I met Mahria. Besides being beautiful and kind, Mahria didn't expect me to spend my entire paycheck (such as it was) on her. She genuinely seemed more concerned about what she could do for me than about what I would do for her. That was a switch. That kind of relationship was new to me.

Mahria was also very committed to her church. She considered the people in her church to be an extension of her own family. That too seemed novel to me. Being curious, and wanting to get the girl, I agreed to go to church with her. I found that the people were friendly enough. The pastor was friendly enough. After awhile, I even started singing in the choir. I wore a robe with a big cross on the front. God had to appreciate that. Maybe this would be my ticket back into God's good graces.

Trying to Gain God's Approval

Three years later, Mahria and I were married on July 6, 1985, at First United Methodist Church of La Puente, California. Like singing in the choir, I thought for sure that marrying a churchgoing woman would bring me closer to God. I thought that God would use Mahria to fill the void in my heart. And, for the better part of a year, it seemed like this would be the case. But, once the newness of married life started to wear off, I began to sense that familiar emptiness returning to my heart and mind.

Frustrated with myself and with God, I thought, *All right. If going to church and singing in the choir aren't enough, if marrying a wonderful woman isn't enough, then maybe I need to get a better job.* I saw a recruitment ad in the local newspaper for the Los Angeles County Sheriff's Department. I had never considered being a cop before I saw that ad. I thought, *What better way to get God's approval than working in a profession in which I get to fight evil and save the world?* Mahria did not share my enthusiasm. I applied anyway.

During the application process, we learned that Mahria was pregnant. I was hired by the Los Angeles County Sheriff's Department on March 11, 1987, and was ready to begin my academy training. I thought for sure that God was smiling on me now. Six days later, on March 17, our first child, Michelle Marie, was born.

I had a beautiful wife. I belonged to a church. I was beginning a great career. And now I had a new baby. What more could God expect of me? I was doing everything I had been told a good person does. He had to approve of me now. I was beginning to see God as good and loving for the first time in many years. Unfortunately, this view would be short-lived.

Michelle was born in the evening. I remember showing her to my dad and hearing him say that he was proud of me. Once I made sure that Mahria and Michelle were okay, I had a little dinner and went home. Needless to say, I was a bit excited. I couldn't sit still, let alone go to sleep. So, around midnight, I called the hospital to check on my family. *My family.* Boy, did that have a great ring to it.

When a nurse answered the phone, I proudly introduced myself as Michelle Miano's daddy. She asked me to wait a minute and put me on hold. Another nurse picked up the line a minute or two later. "Mr. Miano?" she said. "We think you should come back down to the hospital. Michelle isn't doing well. We're not sure what's wrong with her. And Mahria is very sick. You should get here as soon as you can."

A Clenched Fist

To this day, it brings tears to my eyes as I remember the myriad thoughts that went through my mind as I hung up the phone. One thing I recall very clearly is looking up, raising a clenched fist toward the ceiling, and yelling, "Where are You now, God? Do You hate me so much that You're going to hurt my family?"

Michelle spent the first two weeks of her life in the intensive care unit. The list of her medical problems seemed endless, and included a heart murmur, jaundice, underdeveloped kidneys, a curvature of the spine, and several other medical issues. This precious little girl who, just hours before, was declared to be perfectly healthy, was now fighting for her life. And Mahria was suffering from a very high fever and dangerously high blood pressure.

I spent every free moment at the hospital. Since the academy had not yet started, the Sheriff's Department was understanding and gave me the time off I needed. I remember sitting in a rocking chair next to Michelle's bed. I held her in my arms, crying when she cried—wanting to make all of her fear, pain, and discomfort go away. I promised her that I would never let anyone hurt her. And when I said "anyone," I included God.

Michelle's health slowly improved and my little family made it through my time at the academy. But we weren't out of the woods yet.

A Family Under Stress

If work was stressful, my home life was even more so. Michelle's medical problems seemed never ending. She was seeing specialists for almost every major organ of her body. The constant trips to doctor's offices and hospitals—never knowing for sure what was wrong with our baby—put a great deal of strain on my relationship with Mahria. We had moved to the Santa Clarita Valley so I could be closer to work, but we were now far from our families. We weren't going to church. We had no friends. We never went out because we were constantly dealing with Michelle's illnesses.

I think one reason I put so much effort into my work as a deputy sheriff was to dull the pain from everything else that was going on in my life. Controlling the inmates became an outlet for the lack of control I was feeling at home. Mahria had no such outlet. My family was a mess. My marriage was a mess. Work was hardening me to the world and everyone around me. I was even starting to treat Mahria like the inmates I loathed. Throughout it all, I was angry with God. I did everything I could to be a good person—no one could accuse me of not being a hard worker—but no matter what I did, I couldn't shake the feeling that God had turned His back on me.

One night at work, I overheard the sergeant talking to a group of deputies about his faith. Remember, even though I was ticked off at God, I still believed in Him. I walked up to the group and added my two cents to the conversation. "I'm a Christian," I said. "I sing in the choir." The sergeant looked at me and said two words: "That's nice."

I walked away feeling like a complete hypocrite. In my heart, I knew I wasn't really a Christian. I didn't even know what it meant to be a *real* Christian, but I knew I wasn't one. I didn't think prayer would make me a Christian. As far as I was concerned, prayer had never accomplished anything. So, once again I poured over my mental laundry list of things I had done in an attempt to get closer to God. The only thing I could think of that I hadn't yet tried was reading the Bible.

Not being an avid reader, I figured I could just start at the end of the book to see how it all ends. I lived on "Cliff Notes" in high school. So I opened a Bible to the Book of Revelation. I began to read about beasts coming out of the water, dragons, and bowls of judgment. I closed the book thinking, *That's the god I know—always angry about something.* The next month or so was a time of deep reflection and spiritual struggle.

The Surrender

Finally, God brought me to the realization that there was nothing *I* could do to earn His love and acceptance. I could never be good enough to merit a place in heaven. And God allowed me to see that there was yet one thing I had never done in all of my feeble attempts to draw closer to Him. I had never surrendered my life to Him.

The Lord opened my eyes to see that sports had never really been my god. My attempts to fill the so-called void in my heart with Mahria, Michelle, and a career as a deputy sheriff only served to mask the truth about my heart. God showed me that *I* was my god. Up to that point, my interest in Him was only to the extent that it pleased *me*. I wrongly saw God as being responsible for serving me, for making me happy.

There was yet one thing I had never done in all of my feeble attempts to draw closer to God. I had never surrendered my life to Him.

For the first time, I saw my behavior and my attitudes toward God and others not as shortcomings and mistakes, but for what they really were—*sin*. I realized that my sin—even one sin, no matter how slight in my own mind—was enough to warrant His righteous judgment and the sentence of hell for all eternity.

I thought of Jesus dying on the cross for my sin. Once I understood that "the wages of sin is death," I saw His sacrifice in a way that I had never seen it before. His sacrificial death and glorious resurrection was now so much more than the historic event I had learned about as a child in catechism. That horrific, magnificent moment in history was now very personal. It was personal because I now realized that Jesus Christ, God in the flesh, didn't simply die on the cross. He died on the cross for *me*. He loved me so much that He sacrificed His perfect, innocent, sinless life in order to provide *me* with the only way to eternal life.

God was no longer an unknowable entity sitting in yonder heaven. He was *my* God. He was *my* heavenly Father. He loved me enough to send His Son to die on *my* behalf. *My* God was loving, holy, righteous, and just. He extended to me the free gift of eternal life through His Son Jesus Christ —not because I earned it or could ever deserve it, but because He is perfectly gracious and merciful.

Salvation

On September 4, 1988, while lying alone on my bed, I cried out to God to forgive me and save me from my sin. I surrendered control of my life to Jesus Christ as my Lord and Savior. I asked Him to change my life and show me how to live for Him, instead of for myself. And He was and is forever faithful. He heard my prayer and answered, extending to a sinner like me the free gift of eternal life—a gift that is given by the grace of God alone, through faith alone, in Jesus Christ alone.

It is because of my relationship with Jesus Christ— again, a relationship I neither earned nor deserved—that I can, by faith, put on the spiritual armor of God and serve Him with my whole heart.

Having now been qualified to wear both the uniform of the police officer and the armor of God, let me share with you what I have learned of their similarities, whether fighting the physical battle against crime or the spiritual battle against evil. You may or may not wear the law enforcement uniform, but I pray that you see your need to put on the spiritual armor that God provides.

Chapter Three

THE BATTLEFIELD

s human beings living on this planet, every person needs to understand that there is a spiritual war raging between two kingdoms—the kingdoms of good and evil. Like it or not, believe it or not, it is true. The battle is real. And every individual is in the midst of the battlefield.

Our adversary is Satan—in fact, that is the meaning of his name. Satan, the devil, is referred to in the Bible as the "evil one" and "the enemy" (Matthew 13:19,39). He is given many other names and descriptions. He is called a "murderer," the "father of lies," and the "deceiver of the world" (John 8:44; Revelation 12:9). He is the "god of this world" and the "ruler of demons" (2 Corinthians 4:4; Matthew 9:34). Although God is sovereign over all of creation, and Satan has no power or authority over God, God has allowed Satan to be the present ruler of this fallen, earthly kingdom.

Those who place their trust in Jesus Christ as their Savior, however, become part of God's kingdom. Although they still live in the earthly realm, their citizenship is in heaven, where they are assured of spending eternity. Through His sacrificial death on the cross, Christ has already won the eternal victory for those who trust in Him, and His resurrection rendered "powerless him who had the power of death, that is, the devil" (Hebrews 2:14). Those who trust in Jesus Christ no longer need to fear death because they know they have eternal life with Christ.

However, every person on earth faces a daily battle. It is a battle against real spiritual forces that, although already ultimately defeated and condemned, still prowl the earth seeking to torment the people who inhabit this world. While individuals belong to his kingdom, Satan can inflict fatal wounds. Once they move into God's kingdom, however, Satan and his demons can only harass and trouble Christians, tempting them to engage in sinful activity.

Some people may imagine that becoming a Christian makes them exempt from the battle. Do you remember the anti-war protests seen around the country at the onset of the Iraq War? During these protests, which were sometimes referred to as "dead-ins," people would lie motionless in the street trying to represent the death that war would bring to our country. Their idea was to avoid conflict because of its terrible consequences. Instead, we should think of ourselves as being on the front lines of battle—like the brave men and women of our armed forces and the law enforcement community. All human beings are in the battle—but whether we choose to put on our protective gear will determine how well we survive.

So let's now look at this battle in which we find ourselves, and the armor that has been provided for our survival.

The Armor of God

The spiritual armor of God is described in the Book of Ephesians, which was a letter that the apostle Paul wrote to the church at Ephesus while he was imprisoned in Rome. In the letter he refers to himself as "the prisoner of the Lord" and "an ambassador in chains" (Ephesians 3:1; 6:20). Luke, a physician and coworker of Paul's, describes the circumstances of Paul's imprisonment: "[Paul] stayed two full years in his own rented quarters, and was welcoming all who came to him, preaching the kingdom of God, and teaching concerning the Lord Jesus Christ with all openness, unhindered" (Acts 28:30,31).

These verses hardly paint a picture of imprisonment that we would recognize today. The fact that Paul stayed "in his own rented quarters" indicates that he was under house arrest, at his own expense. However, this form of custody included a Roman soldier who guarded Paul around the clock. In all likelihood, Paul was chained to the soldier, like the scenes from movies of old, in which a suspect is handcuffed to a detective who is transporting him from one jurisdiction to another. As I tried to picture the scene of Paul's house arrest, I couldn't help but envision him seated at a candlelit table, writing about the spiritual armor of the believer, and occasionally glancing up at his uniformed guard to gather material for his illustration.

With a soldier's uniform in mind, and inspired by the Holy Spirit, Paul describes this armor of God in Ephesians chapter 6:

> Be strong in the Lord, and in the strength of His might. Put on the full armor of God, so that you will be able to stand firm against the schemes of the devil. For our struggle is not against flesh and blood, but against the rulers, against the powers, against the world forces of this darkness, against the spiritual forces of wickedness in the heavenly places.
>
> Therefore, take up the full armor of God, that you will be able to resist in the evil day, and having done everything, to stand firm. Stand firm therefore, having girded your loins with truth, and having put on the

breastplate of righteousness, and having shod your feet with the preparation of the gospel of peace; in addition to all, taking up the shield of faith with which you will be able to extinguish all the flaming arrows of the evil one. And take the helmet of salvation, and the sword of the Spirit, which is the word of God. (Ephesians 6:10–17)

Before describing the various pieces of equipment, Paul begins by giving his readers a couple of commands and the reason for these marching orders:

> *"Be strong in the Lord and in the strength of His might.*
> *Put on the full armor of God, so that you will be able*
> *to stand firm against the schemes of the devil."*
> *(Ephesians 6:10,11)*

Being "Made" Strong

The first command is to "be strong in the Lord and in the strength of His might." This is not a call to develop our own strength. The command is to be "made" strong in the Lord. In other words, we are commanded to draw from Him all the strength we need to fight the spiritual battles we face. We are to be strong in the strength of *His* might, not our own. King David understood this when he wrote, "Who is the King of glory? The LORD strong and mighty, the LORD mighty in battle" (Psalm 24:8). The Bible assures us that "the battle is the Lord's" (1 Samuel 17:47), and that "the Lord is faithful, and He will strengthen and protect you from the evil one" (2 Thessalonians 3:3).

Just as in the spiritual realm, our strength as peace officers is not our own. I've worked with officers, usually those new to the law enforcement family, who mistakenly thought that now that they wore a gun and a badge they were, by default, physically stronger and possessed more "street smarts" than the criminal element of our society. This phenomenon is commonly known as "The John Wayne Syndrome." I've seen inexperienced cops get themselves into difficult situations in which they relied on what they wrongly believed to be their enhanced physical strength, instead of relying on the legal authority they brought into the situation.

During the academy and patrol training, all peace officers are taught the importance of command presence. I was taught that the manner in which I carried myself and the manner in which I took control of a situation could very well determine whether or not a suspect would choose to fight with me. And at 5'8" and 180 pounds, I quickly learned while working in the county jail that the command presence I possessed, and not my physical prowess, was what deterred inmates from challenging me physically. It was the authority vested in me, allowing me to serve as a deputy sheriff, which caused the inmates to think twice about "taking me on." It was the known consequences for challenging that authority that more often than not kept the inmates from rising up against my fellow deputies and me.

I worked in a jail facility called an "open compound," in which the inmates lived in open barracks, not cells. On any given day, 15 to 20 deputies were tasked with controlling more than 1,000 inmates in this open environment. Even if my fellow deputies and I were each 7' tall and weighed over 300 pounds, there is nothing the handful of us could do, by our own power, to stop 1,000 inmates from taking over the facility if they had a mind to do it. What deterred the inmates from taking such action was the authority by which we supervised the facility and the knowledge of the consequences for challenging our authority.

Good cops recognize their physical and tactical limitations and know that the authority they wield is not based on their own physical or mental attributes. They realize that there will always be someone bigger, stronger, faster, meaner, and more cunning than they are. The peace officer's strength is derived from a higher power—the laws of local, state, and federal governments. Without that *legal* authority, the peace officer would have no more power than the average citizen—or the criminal, for that matter.

Without that legal authority, the peace officer would have no more power than the average citizen —or the criminal, for that matter.

Likewise, we cannot survive the daily spiritual battles of this world by relying on our ability to fight off our spiritual enemies with our own strength and power. As sinful, fallible, mortal human beings, we do not possess the power to withstand Satan and his demonic forces. Just as it would have been complete foolishness for me to walk alone onto the jail compound and challenge 1,000 inmates to a fight, it is likewise foolish to believe that we can take on Satan and his minions on our own.

Our only hope in winning the daily spiritual battles against the enemy is to rely on the spiritual authority vested in us. And that authority is found in none other than Jesus Christ, who declares, "All authority has been given to Me in heaven and on earth" (Matthew 28:18).

Imagine a civilian, claiming to have the authority of a cop, walking into the middle of a domestic dispute or bar fight and declaring, "By the authority vested in me by the laws of this country, I command you to stop what you are doing!" The involved parties would likely look at the civilian and laugh—or, worse, the civilian could himself become a victim. Likewise, those who do not know Jesus Christ as their Savior do not stand a chance in the spiritual battles we all face. Those without a real relationship with Jesus Christ stand alone and unprotected, without power or authority, in the middle of a battleground. And those who know Jesus Christ but insist on fighting the battle in their own strength will also suffer defeat. Only by being strong in *Him* and in the strength of *His might* can we succeed.

Suiting Up

Although our strength comes from Jesus Christ, we are responsible for putting on "the full armor of God." In a sense, the second command explains how we are to carry out the first command. Because the strength we need for the fight is not our own and we are to rely completely on God's strength, power, and might to see us through, we are commanded to suit up with the protective armor He provides.

In the Greek language in which Paul wrote this letter, the word he used for "put on" carries the idea of permanence. So, what Paul is saying is that once you put on the armor of God, you are to wear it for the rest of your life. It's not like a regular suit of clothes that you change every day depending on the weather, or the activity, or the people you plan to be with, or if the clothes get dirty. We are to put on God's armor and keep it on, regardless of the circumstances and regardless of how tough the fight gets. In fact, this is when it's most crucial to keep it on.

The reason we are to rely on God's strength and clothe ourselves with His armor is "so that [we] will be able to stand firm against the schemes of the devil." The Greek word translated as the phrase "to stand firm," when used in a military sense, has the idea of holding a critical position while under attack.

What would we think if we saw our troops in Iraq walking toward Baghdad wearing jeans, T-shirts, and tennis shoes? Or if law enforcement personnel responded to another terrorist attack in our country dressed in khakis and Hawaiian shirts? We would rightly think that there is no way the troops or police officers would be able to hold their positions if attacked by the enemy. We would ask why they weren't in uniform and armed for battle.

We too must be in uniform and prepared for battle. Unless we have on the full armor of God, Paul warns us, we will not be able to stand against the schemes of the devil.

The Schemes of the Devil

What are some of the schemes of the devil? Remember, Satan is referred to in the Bible as the "father of lies." From his first appearance in recorded history, in the Garden of Eden, his primary goal has been to deceive mankind, enticing people to disobey God's commands and to turn away from the one true God. Eve succumbed to his deception, admitting, "The serpent deceived me, and I ate" (Genesis 3:13).

Satan has deceived people in innumerable ways throughout history, enticing them to believe anything but the truth. He has convinced them that there are many gods, that it's foolish to believe there is only one God. He has also deceived people into thinking that only a fool would believe God even exists. The Bible, however, tells us, "The fool has said in his heart, 'There is no God'" (Psalm 14:1). It also says: "Since the creation of the world [God's] invisible attributes, His eternal power and divine nature, have been clearly seen, being understood through what has been made, so that they are without excuse. For even though they knew

God, they did not honor Him as God or give thanks, but they became futile in their speculations, and their foolish heart was darkened" (Romans 1:20,21).

Satan deceives people into thinking that mankind is basically good, and that if a man's good deeds outnumber his sins, he will find himself in heaven one day. Yet the Bible tells us mankind's true state: "The LORD has looked down from heaven upon the sons of men to see if there are any who understand, who seek after God. They have all turned aside, together they have become corrupt; there is no one who does good, not even one" (Psalm 14:2,3). And, regarding our good works earning our place in heaven, the Bible says this: "For by grace you have been saved through faith; and that not of yourselves, it is the gift of God; not as a result of works, so that no one may boast" (Ephesians 2:8,9).

The deceiver convinces people that what they do in secret will remain a secret, whether it is adultery, pornography, theft, the worship of false gods, or any other sin. But the Bible says, "If we had forgotten the name of our God or extended our hands to a strange god, would not God find this out? For He knows the secrets of the heart" (Psalm 44:20,21).

Satan continues to deceive the people of this world by convincing them that God's Law, His Ten Commandments, are, at best, an optional moral code. Worse yet, he convinces people that they are either able to keep God's perfect standard of living or are above God's standards. Or Satan deludes people into believing that they are not accountable to God for violating His Law. Yet the Bible says, "Now we know that whatever the Law says, it speaks to those who are under the Law, so that every mouth may be closed and all the world may become accountable to God; because by the works of the Law no flesh will be justified in His sight; for through the Law comes the knowledge of sin" (Romans 3:19,20).

I was once so deceived. Before I placed my faith in Christ, I believed in a god of my own choosing, a god I had created in my own imagination. I believed that if the good in my life outweighed the bad, God would let me into heaven. I believed that my secret sins were just that—secrets I could keep not only from the people around me, but from God. I believed that I was good—that I was not a thief, a liar, an adulterer, or a murderer. I rationalized the time I stole a pack of gum from the grocery store as nothing more than a childhood indiscretion. I excused the lies I had told as harmless fibs. I justified the lust of my flesh and the lust of my eyes because I never physically cheated on my wife. And I would never have considered myself a murderer, because I never acted upon the hate I harbored in my heart for other people.

If you were a wrestler in the Greco-Roman world and you lost the match, embarrassment and humiliation were the least of your worries.

I was wrong. I was dead wrong. I had violated every aspect of God's Law. Had it not been for Jesus Christ, who died to pay for my sin, I would have faced an eternity in hell. "For this you know with certainty, that no immoral or impure person or covetous man, who is an idolater, has an inheritance in the kingdom of Christ and God. Let no one deceive you with empty words, for because of these things the wrath of God comes upon the sons of disobedience" (Ephesians 5:5,6). It was the realization that hell is exactly what I deserved for violating God's Law, and that I couldn't save myself, which drove me to my knees to ask Him for forgiveness and to save my life. And God was gracious, sparing me from the wrath to come.

Whatever you believe, if it's anything other than trusting in Jesus Christ alone for your salvation, the enemy has succeeded in keeping you from the one true God. Don't fall prey to the schemes of the devil. After all, as Paul so aptly says, we are in a real battle:

> *"For our struggle is not against flesh and blood, but against the rulers, against the powers, against the world forces of this darkness, against the spiritual forces of wickedness in the heavenly places." (Ephesians 6:12)*

Hand-to-Hand Combat

In verse 12, Paul gives us a description of the spiritual battlefield on which we find ourselves. The Greek word he uses to describe this struggle was commonly used for the sport of wrestling in the first century.[1] In other words, Paul has in mind hand-to-hand combat.

Paul grew up in an area where one of the primary sources of entertainment at that time were the games—what we refer to today as the Olympic Games. The games of Paul's day, however, were much different than those we watch every four years. Although, like today, athletic events of 2,000 years ago were filled with pomp and circumstance, it is not melodramatic to say that the games of his day were life-and-death struggles.

Wrestling matches serve as a good example of this truth. If you were a wrestler 2,000 years ago in the Greco-Roman world and you lost the match, embarrassment and humiliation were the least of your worries. It was not uncommon for the loser to have his eyes gouged out as the penalty for his defeat. It was this kind of very real, life-and-death conflict that Paul had in mind when he wrote about the spiritual struggle.

Knowing the Enemy

Paul then reminds us that in this spiritual battle the true enemy is not of this world and is not "flesh and blood." We should always keep in mind that the major battle we are fighting is in the spiritual, not the physical, realm. Martyn Lloyd-Jones, the great British preacher of the last century, wrote, "The beginning of this matter is to realize that we are living in a spiritual realm, a spiritual atmosphere. This world is not only a material one—there is the spiritual element surrounding it and there are forces and spirits which are evil and malign, set against God and everything that is holy."[2]

Although demons can exert influence over what people think and do, no level of demonic influence relieves any person of the responsibility for the sins he or she chooses to commit. The Bible makes that clear: "Let no one say when he is tempted, 'I am being tempted by God'; for God cannot be tempted by evil, and He Himself does not tempt anyone. But each one is tempted when he is carried away and enticed by his own lust.' Then when lust has conceived, it gives birth to sin; and when sin is accomplished, it brings forth death. Do not be deceived, my beloved brethren" (James 1:13–16). No one can legitimately argue that "the devil made me do it." The sin in a person's life is the result of one's own desire to sin, to do the things that go against God's Word and God's will.

For instance, the person who spends time viewing pornographic websites is alone responsible for being involved in such activity. Yet, demonic forces can certainly be at work orchestrating temptation after temptation—maybe through print and other media sources—giving the person ample opportunity to fall prey to his or her own lustful and sinful desires.

So while spiritual forces cannot control us, they can certainly influence us. Our struggle against a supernatural enemy is futile if fought in our own strength. John Calvin writes:

> [Paul] means that our difficulties are far greater than if we had to fight against men. Where we resist human strength, sword is opposed to sword, man contends with man, force is met by force, and skill by skill; but here the case is very different, for our enemies are such as no human power can withstand.

In any battle situation, soldiers will fail if their weapons are not equal to those of their enemy. Likewise, peace officers going out into the field must be properly equipped and protected in order to subdue any criminals and not be overcome. Since our struggle is not against a visible, human enemy, but against an unseen spiritual foe, we cannot prevail in our own strength. By ourselves, our strength is no match for the enemy's. A spiritual battle calls for spiritual battle gear. We must be convinced of this—and properly attired—if we are to succeed. That's why Paul writes:

> *"Therefore, take up the full armor of God, so that you will be able to resist in the evil day, and having done everything, to stand firm." (Ephesians 6:13)*

Stand Firm and Stay Alert!

Paul reminds his readers, and us, that we must be ready for the battle by taking up the *full* armor of God. Each piece of armament is critically important and is necessary for our safety in the midst of the battlefield. It is only by being clothed in God's armor that any of us are able, with God's power, to resist in the evil day. The "evil day" that Paul is referring to is basically every day of human existence since the fall of Adam and Eve. Every day since that tragic moment has been marred by pain, suffering, and death; therefore, every day we must resist the temptation to succumb to evil.

The Scriptures tell us that the way to resist temptation is to draw near to God: "Submit therefore to God. Resist the devil and he will flee from you" (James 4:7). And the apostle Peter wisely counseled, "Be of sober spirit, be on the alert. Your adversary, the devil, prowls around like a roaring lion, seeking someone to devour. But resist him, firm in your faith" (1 Peter 5:8,9).

The battle is real. The enemy is real. The occasional wounds and the promised victories are real. We must stand firm. We must be alert. We must stay vigilant.

Staying alert is critically important to police officers, whether they are working the streets, in the detective bureau, or in the jails. I have learned during my law enforcement career that criminals plan continually for a violent encounter with those behind the badge. While I was working in the county jail system, I occasionally caught inmates practicing "gun takeaways"—techniques for grabbing an officer's gun during a pat-down search, and using it to kill that officer.

Sadly, there have been many instances when peace officers have been killed with their own weapons. On January 18, 2005, Officer James Prince of the Boiling Spring Lakes Police Department, in North Carolina, made the ultimate sacrifice under such tragic circumstances. The "Officer Down Memorial Page" website gives the following account:

Officer Prince was shot and killed with his own service weapon after making a traffic stop…During the stop Officer Prince learned that the suspect was wanted on a probation violation in a neighboring county.

As Officer Prince attempted to arrest the suspect, a struggle ensued. The suspect was able to gain control of the officer's service weapon and shot him three times. Officer Prince was found a short time later by a Southport Police Department officer who had responded to the scene as backup. The suspect later shot at Caswell Beach Police Department and Oak Island Police Department officers who spotted his vehicle. The man was arrested a short time later hiding under a mobile home.[3]

In many other situations, criminals have lured officers into an ambush during foot pursuits or by making false calls for assistance to the police department. When criminals know that the police are on their way, they have ample time to conceal themselves and to assume an advantageous tactical position so they can "get the drop" on the responding officers.

I remember answering a "918/417" call several years ago ("918" is the radio code for a mentally disturbed person, and "417" indicates "a man with a gun"). The caller reported that a man was standing in front of his house, yelling and holding a shotgun.

The call came from a semi-rural area of our jurisdiction, where the roads were dirt and there were no streetlights. My partner and I approached the location in our patrol car as cautiously as possible. We couldn't see the suspect, nor could we hear him yelling. I remember both of us drawing our weapons and holding them on our laps as we drove past a tall, thick hedgerow. I remarked to my partner that the suspect could be anywhere, and if the suspect was on the opposite side of the bushes, we were sitting ducks.

A short time later, we located the suspect in his home and took him into custody without incident. And we found his shotgun, loaded with rifle slugs—a large, solid ball of lead that could penetrate a concrete block wall.

Although this particular call ended well, as my partner and I talked to one of the suspect's neighbors, the hair on the back of our necks stood on end. The neighbor told us that he heard us drive down the road. When he looked outside, he could see the suspect standing behind the hedgerow, pointing his shotgun at our patrol car on the opposite side of the bushes. The neighbor could hear the suspect say, "*Pow, pow, pow,*" as we drove by. It was only by God's grace that the suspect didn't fire the shotgun into our patrol car. Because of the devastating nature of the round—which could penetrate a car door like a warm knife cuts through butter—the suspect could have killed us both with one shot.

We need to remain alert because—whether we are aware he exists or not—our spiritual enemy is constantly looking for an opportunity to attack. He is well versed in disarming us. He is not above lying in wait to ambush us. So we must always be prepared. The battlefield is closer than the world around you. It is even closer than the peaceful confines of your own home. *You* are part of the battlefield. Don't go into battle unarmed. Don't take to the field poorly equipped. Take up the full armor of God so you can stand firm against the enemy's attacks. Get suited and armed for battle. Be alert!

Chapter Four

THE BELT OF TRUTH

*"Stand firm therefore, having girded your loins
with truth..." (Ephesians 6:14a)*

A s Paul begins the discussion of the armor of God, he reiterates the command to "stand firm." Using repetition to emphasize its importance, he reaffirms the mandate to stand, along with the practical application of suiting up for battle. In his call to stand firm, Paul has in mind the Roman soldier. Like the peace officer, the soldier, sailor, marine, or airman of today, the Roman soldier "was to be the kind of person who could be relied upon, when under pressure, to stand fast and not give way."[4]

The Equipment

So, what are these individual pieces that make up the spiritual armor? There are six pieces of equipment altogether. The first five are defensive in nature. The sixth has a dual role—both offensive and defensive.

The first item Paul mentions is the "belt of truth." The Roman soldier's main piece of clothing was the tunic—a

53

simple, square-shaped garment with openings for the head and arms. It was very loose fitting, which was a hindrance during hand-to-hand combat. So, the soldier wore a sturdy leather belt around his waist and gathered the tunic into the belt so it wouldn't get in his way. The belt therefore served to keep him from stumbling. It also held his weapon.

To bring Paul's illustration into contemporary times, men and women in law enforcement—our frontline soldiers for home defense—wear belts that are an important part of their uniforms.

What most civilians would call a gun belt is better known as a "Sam Browne" belt in the law enforcement community. Named after Sir Samuel Browne of the British Army, the Sam Browne belt came into existence around 1861. As a major assigned to a regiment in India, Browne lost his left arm while charging and capturing a rebel gun position.

With only one arm, he could no longer carry his sword comfortably, especially when on a horse. So, he designed a belt to hold his sword. The belt consisted of two leather straps—one around the waist and one that crossed over the right shoulder, with a D-ring for the sword. A holster was soon added to minimize the number of "A.D.'s" (accidental discharges) that were fairly common with sidearms in those days. Over the years, the Sam Browne, as it's used by law enforcement, has evolved to the belt you see worn today by peace officers around the country.

I remember the first time I put on this belt in the academy. After a day of marching and running, my back and my head were killing me. But the more I wore the belt (I even wore it around the house to help me get accustomed to it), the less my body hurt. Something I learned early on was that the tighter I wore the belt, the less stress and strain it put on my back. It was also easier to draw the various weapons from the belt when it was secure around my waist. I got so used to it that it became part of me. I wouldn't think of working uniformed patrol without it.

When a soldier "girds his loins" by putting on his belt, he is saying, in effect, "I'm ready to fight. I'm committed to the battle." The same is true for the peace officer. A cop who puts on his or her Sam Browne is making a commitment to go into the field, handle the calls, and anything else society might dish out. How can we possibly stand firm? How can we claim to be prepared for battle if we're not committed to the task at hand? Likewise, if we are not committed to a life marked by truthfulness, then we are going into spiritual battles improperly armed and susceptible to attacks of temptation from the enemy. If truth is not securely wrapped around us, we will stumble.

Having been a cop most of my adult life, I feel comfortable saying that a peace officer without integrity has no business wearing the badge.

Paul uses the word "truth" in such a way as to give it a couple of different applications. The truth Paul is referring to is the truth of God's Word (the Bible), but he also means we should have an attitude of truthfulness. In order to effectively withstand the spiritual dark forces of this world, we must be equipped with the truth. And it's not enough to simply know or possess the truth; we must have a genuine commitment to the truth.

Having been a cop most of my adult life, I feel very comfortable saying that a peace officer without integrity has no business wearing the badge. Strong words, I know, but true nonetheless. I make such a strong assertion fully aware that peace officers are drawn from the same fallible human race from which every other profession draws its people. I understand that otherwise honest men and women can make mistakes that can lead to momentary breeches in their integrity. And I'm also intimately aware of the day-to-day temptations peace officers face—temptations to make truth a relative term, to blur the line between truth and error, and to move that fine line in order to meet the perceived needs of the moment.

Integrity and Car Seats

Like every other street cop, I've faced such temptation many times during my career. I remember one night my partner, Deputy Bryan White, and I faced such a test. We were working near Castaic Lake, an unincorporated area of northern Los Angeles County. We were assigned to the early morning shift, and the canyon roads around the lake often provided interesting encounters and arrests.

As we drove up the canyon road on the east side of the lake, we saw a lowered mini-truck approaching us. The vehicle was coming out of a remote and otherwise uninhabited area. As the truck passed us, we noticed two guys inside who looked too young to be out so late at night. So, for that reason, along with a host of noticeable vehicle violations, we stopped the truck. When we approached the occupants we saw that the two bucket seats inside the vehicle belonged in a car, not a truck. As the occupants got out of the vehicle, we noticed that not only did the seats not belong in the truck, they were not even bolted to the floorboard. We could also see a number of tools strewn about the vehicle's interior.

The driver claimed to have purchased the seats, but he could not produce a receipt. The two also had conflicting stories about why they were out so late and why they were coming out of a canyon nowhere near their homes. We arrested them for reasonable cause-burglary. We were convinced that a crime had occurred. We were convinced that these two guys burglarized someone's vehicle and stole the seats. We just didn't know who the victim of the crime was.

We transported the two suspects to the station and spent the better part of the night trying to convince the watch commander to sign-off on what we thought was a good hook. Once we had the watch commander's approval and booked the suspects, it was time to book the evidence —including the two bucket seats. As Bryan and I carried the seats to the outside evidence locker, a piece of paper fell out of the pocket of the seat I was carrying. I put the seat on the ground, picked up the piece of paper, and unfolded it. I looked closely at the paper, hoping against hope that the print would change before my eyes. But it didn't. The piece of paper was a receipt from a pick-a-part place for two bucket seats.

After all the work we did to honestly and professionally put together a good felony arrest, we knew that the small piece of paper that had fallen out of the seat meant that our good police work was for naught. We both knew, though neither of us suggested this to the other, that if that piece of paper conveniently disappeared no one would be the wiser and our arrest would stick. Bryan is not only a brother behind the badge, but also a fellow Christian. We looked at each other, and—without saying a word—we knew what we had to do. We had to go back to the watch commander's office, show him the receipt, and ask him to approve the release of the two suspects we had spent so much time convincing him we should book on felony charges.

Needless to say, the watch commander wasn't very pleased—although he should have been. It wasn't sloppy police work, but integrity that resulted in the release of the suspects. Bryan and I left the station parking lot feeling good about our decision. We couldn't help but laugh, though, as we drove by the front of the station. There sat our two suspects, waiting for a ride (we had also impounded their truck), making themselves comfortable in the two bucket seats that we had thought were stolen.

Truth Can Be Uncomfortable

Helmut Thielicke, a professor of theology at the University of Heidelberg until he was ousted by the Nazis in 1940, once said, "The avoidance of one small fib...may be a stronger confession of faith than a whole 'Christian philosophy' championed in lengthy, forceful discussion." In other words, a commitment to truthfulness speaks volumes about the depth, breadth, and genuineness of one's faith. If Christians are going to stand firm in their faith, then they must gird themselves with the belt of truthfulness—living lives marked by integrity.

As I mentioned earlier, I've worn my Sam Browne belt for so many years that I've grown used to having it around my waist. But that doesn't mean it is always comfortable. Wearing a fully equipped belt weighing several pounds, for eight to sixteen hours straight, in temperatures topping 100 degrees, while repeatedly climbing in and out of a vehicle, or while chasing a fleeing suspect through a darkened alley, can be uncomfortable and tiring. Holding tightly to the truth, day in and day out, regardless of the conditions, can likewise be uncomfortable and tiring.

But, just as police officers would never think of taking off their Sam Browne during a shift or in the middle of a chase, followers of Jesus Christ should never consider taking off the belt of truth. It doesn't matter how uncomfortable standing for the truth may become as we navigate through our tour of duty here on earth. To take off the belt of truth—to set aside the truth of God's Word and personal integrity—serves but one purpose: to expose you to temptation, sin, and attacks from your spiritual enemy, Satan.

The Ultimate Source of Truth

In order to live a life marked by truthfulness, one must recognize that truth is not a relative term. It is never contradictory; there cannot be "my truth" versus "your truth." There is only one source of pure truth. It is not found in science or philosophy. It is not found in situational ethics or in the judicial systems of the world. God alone, the one true God, is the source of truth. And He has given us His truth through His written Word—the Bible. D. L. Moody once said, "God did not give us the Scriptures to increase our knowledge, but to change our lives." And John Wesley understood this when he said, "I want to know one thing— the way to heaven...God Himself has condescended to teach the way. He [has written] it down in a book. O give me that Book! At any price, give me the Book of God!"

Men like Moody and Wesley, and Christians throughout the ages, confidently turned to the Bible as the ultimate source of truth. Their unabashed, unashamed commitment and submission to what the Bible teaches came not from a blind faith, but from reading and believing what the Bible says about itself. If you are not a Christian, I encourage you to take the time to read the Bible and honestly investigate its claims. All who are looking for truth will find it: "Your word is truth" (John 17:17).

Jesus says, "If you continue in My word, then you are truly disciples of Mine; and you will know the truth, and the truth will make you free" (John 8:31,32). But Jesus is so much more than a purveyor of truth. Jesus Christ, God in the flesh, can never be relegated to merely a "good teacher" or a "wise prophet." No matter how hard mankind may try, there is no changing the fact that He *is* truth. Jesus says, "I am the way, and the truth, and the life; no one comes to the Father, but through Me" (John 14:6).

Wearing the belt of truth means having a genuine commitment to the truth of God's Word. And that kind of commitment is not seen in how much we talk about our commitment to God's Word, but in how much time we actually spend reading, studying, meditating on, and applying God's Word to our lives. Ray Stedman writes, "It is hard to understand Christians who think they can live a Christian life without ever reading their Bibles. It is impossible. Our memories do not retain and maintain what we need to know. We are built in such a way that we need refreshment and need to be reminded—again and again."

> *We should not enter the spiritual battlefield blindly. Rather, we should enter the fray aided by the light of God.*

The Light of Truth

One of the pieces of equipment I wear on my Sam Browne is a flashlight. It's small but powerful. Having spent a good portion of my patrol career working after dark, I wouldn't think of approaching a car or searching a building without my flashlight. It's just too dangerous to enter a location blindly. Likewise, we should not enter the spiritual battlefield blindly. Rather, we should enter the fray aided by the light of God.

The Bible tells us that Jesus is "the true Light which, coming into the world, enlightens every man" (John 1:9).

Jesus Himself said, "I am the Light of the world; he who follows Me will not walk in darkness, but will have the Light of life" (John 8:12).

There is only one light powerful enough to penetrate the darkest recesses of the human heart. It is the light of Jesus Christ and His Word. It would be foolish for a cop to go into a pitch-black building with a single candle in his hand, knowing that he had a flashlight on his belt as powerful as tens of thousands of candles. It is no less foolish for a person to try to navigate through the spiritual darkness of this world by relying on the insufficient candle power of his own understanding, when God has given us all the light we will ever need through the truth of His Word: "Your word is a lamp to my feet and a light to my path" (Psalm 119:105).

It is no coincidence that Paul listed the belt of truth before the other pieces of spiritual armor. Without first being grounded in the truth, without first being fully committed to the essential beliefs of the Christian faith, it is all but impossible to don, let alone rightly employ, the other critical pieces of spiritual armament.

So, put on the belt of truthfulness. Daily wear the belt of God's truth. Memorize and mediate upon the truth of God's Word, so that whenever you need its light, Scripture will be ever-present—deep in your heart, at the front of your mind, and on the tip of your tongue. Be known as a person of integrity, one who can be counted on to tell the truth regardless of the circumstances and regardless of the consequences. You will be far better equipped to stand firm and fight in spiritual battles.

Chapter Five

THE BREASTPLATE OF RIGHTEOUSNESS

"...and having put on the breastplate of righteousness."
(Ephesians 6:14b)

Next in Paul's list of armament is the "breastplate of righteousness." Roman soldiers wore a piece of equipment called the "thorax." According to John MacArthur, it was "a tough, sleeveless piece of armor that covered his full torso. It was often made of leather or heavy linen, onto which were sewn overlapping slices of animal hooves or horns or pieces of metal. Some were made of large pieces of metal molded or hammered to conform to the body."[5] The purpose of the breastplate is obviously to protect the vital organs.

Body Armor

The contemporary equivalent to the breastplate is what many would refer to as the "bullet-proof vest." It is more appropriately referred to as a "bullet-resistant" or "anti-ballistic" vest. Within the law enforcement community, it is simply called the "vest" or "body armor."

Body armor did not become widely available to law enforcement personnel until 1975. At that time, fifteen urban law enforcement agencies agreed to field-test body armor made of a newly invented material—Kevlar. Body armor is now standard equipment for the peace officer.

"A History of Body Armor" describes how it works:

> When a handgun bullet strikes body armor, it is caught in a "web" of very strong fibers. These fibers absorb and disperse the impact energy that is transmitted to the vest from the bullet, causing the bullet to deform or "mushroom." Additional energy is absorbed by each successive layer of material in the vest, until such time as the bullet has been stopped. Because the fibers work together both in the individual layer and with other layers of material in the vest, a large area of the garment becomes involved in preventing the bullet from penetrating. This also helps in dissipating the forces which can cause nonpenetrating injuries (what is commonly referred to as "blunt trauma") to internal organs.[6]

More Than a Dirty T-Shirt

In determining what kind of righteousness Paul has in mind for this breastplate, we have three types from which to choose. The first, and most unlikely, is self-righteousness. Trusting in our own righteousness is like going into battle expecting a dirty T-shirt to stop a flaming spear or a speeding bullet. While most of us think we're pretty good, the Bible tells us that, in God's eyes, "all our righteous deeds are like a filthy garment" (Isaiah 64:6).

Whenever I give a talk about the armor of God, I invite someone to join me in front of the group. As the volunteer comes up to the stage, I toss the person a T-shirt that has served me well for many years. I've used the T-shirt to polish my boots and brass and to clean my duty weapon. Needless to say, the T-shirt is a "filthy garment."

The T-shirt is so dirty that I do not ask the person to put it on. Instead, I have him hold the T-shirt up in front of him while I explain to the audience that I'm going to conduct a brief experiment. I say to everyone that—with the help of my volunteer—I'm going to test the stopping power of my dirty T-shirt. To accomplish this, my plan is to remove my duty weapon from its holster and fire a single round into the chest of my volunteer. It's not unusual for my unwitting assistant's demeanor to change at this point.

I then turn to the person holding my T-shirt and ask him if he thinks the T-shirt will stop my bullet. Invariably, the person firmly and expressively shakes his head. I explain to the audience that just like my volunteer wisely understands that a dirty T-shirt won't stop a speeding bullet, neither should any of us rely on our own righteousness or perceived goodness to serve as a breastplate or body armor, protecting us from the enemy in the spiritual battle.

It is this refusal to rely on self-righteousness that differentiates biblical Christianity from every other religion in the world today. Every other major religion has, as part of its basic doctrine, the need for followers to earn or work their way to heaven, if they even believe in the concept of eternal life. The Bible tells us the reason people believe this: "Not knowing about God's righteousness and seeking to establish their own, they did not subject themselves to the righteousness of God" (Romans 10:3). In these other religions, good works or righteous acts are considered necessary for one to receive a place in heaven. This is not the case for the Christian, as the Bible so clearly teaches.

Followers of Jesus Christ receive the gift of eternal life only by God's grace—by His unmerited (unearned) favor.

There is nothing that any person can do to earn a place in heaven.

As I have often shared with others, if there was anything I could do to earn eternal life, then Jesus Christ died in vain. If I could ever be good enough or work hard enough to be allowed entrance into heaven, then there was absolutely no need for God to come to earth, taking the form of human flesh in the person of Jesus Christ, and die such a horrible death on the cross on my behalf. And if God *needs* my partnership in the salvation process, if He needs my help through my good works to secure my place in heaven, then He is no longer sovereign—I am. And this is simply *not* what the Bible teaches. God alone is sovereign. God alone saves the sinner from eternal punishment in hell. Consider the following verses:

> The wages of sin is death, but the free gift of God is eternal life in Christ Jesus our Lord. (Romans 6:23)

> By grace you have been saved through faith; and that not of yourselves, it is the gift of God; not as a result of works, so that no one may boast. (Ephesians 2:8,9)

> He saved us, not on the basis of deeds which we have done in righteousness, but according to His mercy. (Titus 3:5)

The next option in the kind of righteousness Paul is referring to is the righteousness we receive from Christ. Because Jesus alone lived a sinless life, He alone is righteous (has right standing before God). When we admit that we can do nothing to save ourselves and we humbly place our faith in Christ, God applies His righteousness to our account. So when God looks at us, He sees the righteousness of Christ. But that can't be what Paul is referring to here. I think John MacArthur says it best when he writes, "We cannot put on what God has already clothed us with. We are permanently dressed in that righteousness, throughout our lives on earth and throughout eternity."[7]

The third possibility, and the kind of righteousness I believe Paul is referring to, is the kind of righteousness that is seen in the practical, day-to-day godliness of the true believer. And that godliness is made visible to the world, and to our enemies in the spiritual realm, through our righteous thoughts and deeds.

Just as putting on the belt was a sign of a Roman soldier's commitment to battle, so too is donning the breastplate. And with the breastplate comes a commitment to obedience—to live in obedience to God's commands and to the truth of His Word. It also signals a commitment to imitate the righteousness of Christ, in keeping with what Paul previously said in Ephesians 5:1: "Therefore be imitators of God, as beloved children."

Part of the strength of the Roman soldier's breastplate was the fact that the protective layers of material overlapped, making it more difficult for the weapons of the enemy to penetrate the armor. What adds to the bullet-resistant nature of Kevlar body armor is the fact that there are several layers of material that compose the vest panel. Without Kevlar, the core material, the vest would be little more than a shirt.

We can consider the various layers of the vest as the righteousness that is shown by our godly living. Over time, as we grow in our faith and spiritual maturity, layers are added to our protective vest, to our breastplate. The more layers we have, the more protection we have. The more we live godly lives, the less likely that the schemes of the devil will be able to penetrate the armor—injuring our heart, crushing our spirits, and damaging our testimony.

The Vest Must Be Worn

As a patrol deputy, I've seen a number of other deputies carry their vests to their radio cars and put them on the front passenger seats. They don't wear their vests. They argue that the weather is too hot or the area where they work is so quiet and "safe" that they don't believe they need it. This is a very dangerous mindset.

Officer Glen Gaspar of the Honolulu Police Department made the ultimate sacrifice early in 2003, while trying to apprehend a suspect wanted for attempted murder. Officer Gaspar's sacrifice makes him a hero worthy of our respect and admiration. Although I would never minimize the sacrifice of a fallen hero, the circumstances surrounding Officer Gaspar's death serve to illustrate an important spiritual point. On December 8, 2003, the Associated Press reported that Officer Gaspar was not wearing a bullet-resistant vest when he was shot.

The AP article included the court testimony of Lt. William Kato, supervisor for the plainclothes unit to which Officer Gaspar belonged. Lt. Kato's testimony is described as follows:

> Kato's testimony answered a question the Honolulu Police Department has skirted since the shooting nine months ago: Was Gaspar wearing his bulletproof vest?
>
> After the shooting, Chief Lee Donohue refused to answer that question, only reiterating departmental policy that "clearly states that officers assigned to enforcement or field patrol duties shall wear body armor while engaged in those duties."

Kato said the vests were avoided by the plain-clothes officers because they "are quite thick, and if you wear them with aloha shirts, it would be quite obvious to anyone out there that you are wearing something under your aloha shirt."[8]

Would Officer Gaspar have survived his deadly encounter had he worn his bullet-resistant vest that fateful day? I don't know. Would wearing a bullet-resistant vest have improved his chances for survival? Depending on where the fatal round struck his body, it is certainly possible.

Sometimes I think Christians enter into the spiritual battle with a mindset similar to that of a peace officer who chooses not to wear a bullet-resistant vest while working the field. We look at living a holy and godly life as too cumbersome, too heavy for the climate we've chosen to live in, or just not necessary. Or, we place too much confidence in our own abilities to avoid dangerous confrontations. So we carry our righteousness under our arms, just so people will think we have it, but we refuse to put it on. We refuse to live the righteous life we want people around us to believe we live—the life God calls us to live.

Sadly, I have talked to peace officers over the years who think they can completely avoid violent confrontations by being lax in their approach to police work. They think that if they just park under a tree and wait for the next call, they will lessen the possibility of getting into a confrontation (verbal or otherwise), or having to take some form of decisive and forceful action. Officers with this mindset are a danger to themselves and to others, particularly their fellow officers. Officers with this mindset are actually at greater risk of injury or death than peace officers who are actively engaged in doing the job—knowing that such work requires them to take certain reasonable risks to safely and professionally protect and serve.

Christians who refuse to don the breastplate of righteousness are equally in danger—in danger of falling prey to Satan's schemes, in danger of being caught off-guard by temptation and wounded as the spinning hot lead of sin pierces their hearts. Satan, our spiritual enemy, is just waiting for us to drop our guard, to become complacent, to set aside our commitment to live a righteous and godly life so that he can attack and inflict as much spiritual damage as possible.

The bruises serve as poignant reminders of the danger the officers were in and the protective ability of their body armor.

Officer Kevin Ford of the Boston Police Department is one officer who came to appreciate the protective power of his bullet-resistant vest. On February 10, 2004, Officer Ford, who is part of the BPD's elite Entry and Apprehension Team (I would love to serve on a team whose name is the acronym "EAT"), was making a high-risk entry into a location when a .45 caliber round came through the wooden door and struck his vest near his abdomen. Despite being hit by what probably felt like a Barry Bonds swing of a baseball bat, Officer Ford continued to enter the location with the rest of his team and apprehended the armed suspect. You have to respect a guy like that. Officer Ford sounds like a "cop's cop."

The *Boston Herald* reported on Officer Ford's critical incident, which included the following reaction of one of Officer Ford's supervisors:

> "It was like being hit with a Pedro Martinez fastball," said Lt. Robert E. O'Toole, commander of the elite Entry and Apprehension Team tapped by state police

drug detectives to clear the way for their execution of a high-risk warrant...in the city's South End.

"My heart was in my throat until I looked at Kevin (in the hospital) and he showed me this...bruise and he laughed," O'Toole said. "I didn't know whether to kiss him or kill him."[9]

Bruises Bring Maturity

Over the years, I have seen photographs of the bruises left on peace officers' bodies from the impact of a round against a bullet-resistant vest. I've also talked with officers who have experienced such an impact firsthand. Without exception, the officers would much rather be bruised than seriously wounded or killed. The bruises serve as very poignant reminders of the danger the officers were in at that moment and the protective ability of their body armor. The bruises also serve to provide all the convincing they will ever need to continue wearing their body armor while on duty.

Wearing the breastplate of righteousness—that is, living a godly life by faith in Jesus Christ—is not a guarantee that you will never be shot at by our spiritual enemy. It is not a guarantee that you will not be hit and even wounded when Satan or his minions attack. It is not a guarantee that you will not suffer pain and discomfort when the enemy strikes. But like the peace officer who dons a bullet-resistant vest, your chances of enduring such an attack are so much greater if you are wearing the breastplate of righteousness.

If you do get hit while wearing your spiritual vest, the bruises caused by such an impact serve not only as reminders of the attack, but also as points of remembrance that will help you mature in your faith. Peace officers who have been involved in shootings, particularly shootings that resulted in injury to themselves or a partner, are forever changed by the experience. The positive changes can include a maturing in the way an officer approaches the job—tactically, physically, and mentally. The same is true for Christians who have endured the enemy's attacks, taking a few rounds to the vest along the way. The experiences prepare them for the possible violent spiritual confrontations in the future. The experiences educate Christians about the tactics of the enemy, equipping them to help others through their own dangerous spiritual encounters.

So, if you're going to survive the spiritual battles that we all face day to day, if you are going to avoid falling prey to sinful temptations, then you had better "vest up," as we say in the law enforcement community. Wear the breastplate of righteousness as one ready for battle.

Chapter Six

SHOES FITTED WITH READINESS

"And having shod your feet with the preparation
of the gospel of peace." (Ephesians 6:15)

V erse 15 gives us the next piece of armament. In this verse, Paul has in mind a passage from the Book of Isaiah: "How lovely on the mountains are the feet of him who brings good news, who announces peace and brings good news of happiness, who announces salvation, and says to Zion, 'Your God reigns!'" (Isaiah 52:7). Paul refers again to this verse in his letter to the Romans: "How will they preach unless they are sent? Just as it is written, 'How beautiful are the feet of those who bring good news of good things!'" (Romans 10:15).

Traction and Preparation

The Roman soldiers of Paul's day wore what could be best described as half boots, called *caliga*. According to R. Kent Hughes, "It was an open-toed leather boot with a heavily nail-studded sole which was tied to the ankles and shins with straps."[10] We shouldn't think of these shoes as running cleats, with their small, thin spikes. These were more like football or baseball cleats, which are thicker and heavier. The purpose of these crudely designed, thicker spikes was to provide the wearer with extra traction. The *caliga* were made for marching and standing one's ground, not for running away.

William Hendriksen, in his commentary on this piece of spiritual battle gear, writes the following:

> One important reason for Julius Caesar's success as a general was the fact that his men wore military shoes that made it possible for them to cover long distances in such short periods that again and again the enemies were caught off guard, having deceived themselves into thinking that they still had plenty of time to prepare an adequate defense. In the victories won by Alexander the Great this same factor had played an important role. Accordingly, proper footwear spells readiness.[11]

Most peace officers wear sturdy boots when they're working patrol. Some wear a steel-toed boot to protect their toes from being stomped on by a suspect or for added power when kicking in a door. The boot of choice has a thick, rubberized, oil-resistant sole that helps to avoid slipping on wet or slick surfaces. Most boots of this type also have extra support for the heel and ankle.

Like the *caliga*, the boots worn by most officers are not designed to help anyone win a track meet, although we often find ourselves chasing after people while wearing our boots. Rather, they are designed to help us stand our ground in a fight or to help us gain entry into places criminals might not want us to go. They also make a formidable weapon against a suspect when the suspect's actions dictate that level of force. Although the work boot needs to be sturdy, it must also be comfortable. Officers have to be able to wear their boots for as much as 16 hours at a time without the hindrance of distracting pain in their feet.

The Greek word that is translated as "preparation" in some Bible versions is better understood to mean "readiness." As believers in Jesus Christ, as people who are at peace *with* God because we have received the free gift of salvation through His Son Jesus Christ, we must always be at the ready to share the same good news—the peace *of* God—with those who do not know such peace. And when we find ourselves facing an attack from the enemy, an onslaught from the devil and his cronies, we must be prepared, ever-ready to stand firm with our feet covered by God's peace, firmly planted and, if necessary, ready to march headlong into the fight.

I like what R. Kent Hughes, one of my favorite authors, wrote. He said, "Those who first have peace *with* God, and then the corollary peace *of* God girding their feet are powerful soldiers in the spiritual battle. No matter what the enemy throws at them, no matter what move the enemy makes, they hold their ground."[12]

Dangers of Being Barefoot

On January 17, 1994, at 4:30 a.m., I was working an early morning traffic car in Santa Clarita, California. The night had been relatively quiet, and, if my memory serves me right, it was unusually warm for January. I received a call to assist the car working the Castaic area on a possible attempted suicide call. Several units rolled because the call indicated that the manner in which the person was planning to kill herself was with a shotgun. The word "possible" meant the desk wasn't sure what we were going to run into when we got to the location. It turned out that the woman was just mad at her boyfriend and really had no intention of killing herself with the shotgun that was in the house.

Once the situation was resolved, we walked out of the house and got back into our cars. As I started the engine, I immediately felt myself driving backward and up onto the sidewalk. *Tony, you knucklehead,* I thought, *put the car in drive, not reverse.* I looked at my dashboard to discover that although my car was moving, it was still in park. And then the ground *really* started to shake.

Having lived in Southern California most of my life, I was very familiar with earthquakes. I could tell this was a big one. The rest of the deputies who were with me simultaneously came to the same conclusion, evidenced by the fact that we all jumped out of our cars and ran to the middle of the street at the same time.

> *I looked at my dashboard to discover that although my car was moving, it was still in park. Then the ground really started to shake.*

As the earth shook, we could see transformers exploding throughout the city. To the south, a bluish glow surrounded the peaks of the Santa Monica Mountains, which separate the Santa Clarita and San Fernando Valleys. Electrical explosions and fires already burning in the San Fernando Valley were causing the glow. We would later learn that we were a mere seven miles northeast of the quake's epicenter in Northridge.

Once the ground stopped shaking, we all got back into our cars and raced south on the I-5 Freeway to Santa Clarita. We had critical facilities to check—places like chemical plants and city government buildings, not to mention the two dams within our jurisdiction. I was the first car in line as we headed down the freeway at about 90 mph. It wasn't long before my car was airborne, having crossed the first break in the freeway. Fortunately for me, the drop was only a foot or so. I got on the radio to let the other units behind me know that we should slow down, since the freeway south of us might not be there anymore. Tragically, this was the case. Officer Clarence Wayne Dean, an LAPD motor officer, died when his motorcycle plunged from the end of a fallen freeway overpass, forty feet to the ground below.

When the call came out that an LAPD motor officer had gone off the I-14 Freeway overpass, we were told that no one could get to him from the south because of the damage to the freeway. Assuming that the I-5 Freeway was still intact, I got on the radio and advised that I was rolling "Code-3" (with lights and siren on), headed south hoping to reach Officer Dean. I made my way around the cars and trucks that were stopped on the freeway. I saw a California Highway Patrol unit stopping traffic up ahead.

I assumed the officer was monitoring our radio frequencies and was stopping traffic for me, so I could get to Officer Dean quicker. But as I got close to the CHP officer, he jumped in front of my car, waving his hands in the air, yelling, "Stop!" He saved my life. Unbeknown to me, the I-5 Freeway had also collapsed just a mile south of there. Had it not been for that CHP officer, I likely would have lost my life the same way Officer Dean had lost his.

Throughout that morning, as we checked various facilities and worked with the Fire Department to pull people out of damaged buildings, the dispatcher periodically got on the radio to give us updates as to the situation in our valley and the rest of Southern California. One message that caught my attention was the local hospital's request for podiatrists (foot doctors). Apparently, the emergency room was inundated with people whose feet were cut and otherwise injured by broken glass and debris.

Those who live outside of earthquake country may not realize that a key to earthquake preparedness is having a pair of shoes next to the bed. This way, when the ground begins to shake in the middle of the night, and you jump out of bed startled, you are able to cover your feet before running out of the bedroom. As was apparent by the number of foot injuries, most Southern Californians did not heed this advice. And, I would suspect that there were many more people immediately after the quake, particularly those who had hurt their feet, who began to leave a pair of shoes beside their beds. I would also suspect that today, ten years later, most of those same people have long since forgotten the practice and run the risk of hurting their feet whenever the earth shakes again.

I think it is safe to assume that most people would not intentionally run through broken glass in their bare feet. In fact, we look at people funny when they walk over burning coals in their bare feet. We wouldn't work barefooted in a construction site, where we could step on stray nails or have tools dropped on our toes. Yet, how often do we stumble into spiritual battles barefooted? How often do we shirk our responsibility to stand firm and share our faith because the sin in our lives or our lack of spiritual maturity keeps us from living in obedience to God?

Or, how often do we know in our hearts that we should share the gospel with the person in front of us, but we cower and miss the opportunity because we don't feel like we're prepared or ready to share? If we claim to know Jesus Christ as our Lord and Savior, and we are not actively engaged in sharing the gospel with those with whom we come in contact, we are sinning against Him and are without excuse.

Ready to Kick Doors

When I was a member of our station's Gang Unit, we served a lot of search warrants. Sometimes our entries into premises required a simple "knock and notice." There were other times when we had to use more forceful measures to gain entry. Looking back on those intense moments when my team approached a door, I can just imagine the response from my partners and my supervisor if I was called upon to kick a door, but I had to ask them to wait because I left my boots in the car.

One of the most dangerous places a peace officer ever stands is in a doorway (open or closed). That is not the time to leave your partner or your team waiting while you run back to the car to grab a piece of equipment you should have been wearing in the first place. There would be no excuse for my lack of preparedness in a situation such as this. The same is true for the Christian's faith. If you find yourself in a situation in which you have an opportunity to share the gospel, or if someone asks you about your relationship with Jesus Christ, that is not the time to say, "Sorry. Can you come back tomorrow? I'm not ready to talk to you today."

If you are going to successfully navigate life's trials, if you are going to experience victories in the spiritual battles all around you, if you are going to keep from missing opportunities to share the good news of Jesus Christ with those who will perish without Him, then you had better get your boots on! First, you need to be equipped for battle by being at peace *with* God, which comes only through submitting to Jesus Christ as the Lord and Savior of your life.

Then you need to be equipped by being ready to share the peace *of* God—the gospel of Jesus Christ—whenever the opportunity arises. As a Christian on this spiritual battlefield, you are called to rescue others from the grasp of the enemy. To do so, you must "always being ready to make a defense to everyone who asks you to give an account for the hope that is in you, yet with gentleness and reverence" (1 Peter 3:15).

If, as a follower of Jesus Christ, you consider yourself unprepared, not ready to share the gospel, what will you do today to prepare? More important, what will you do today to share—to share the hope that is already in you, the good news of Jesus Christ? Stop thinking about it and start doing it! German theologian Dietrich Bonhoeffer, who was executed for his involvement in a plot to overthrow Hitler, said, "Actions spring not from thought, but from a readiness for responsibility."

If you are a Christian, it is not a matter of whether or not you *will be* given the responsibility to share the gospel with the world. It is simply a matter of obedience. Will you obey the Lord Jesus Christ and accept the responsibility you have already been given? Put your boots on and share your faith!

Chapter Seven

THE SHIELD
OF FAITH

*"In addition to all, taking up the shield of faith with
which you will be able to extinguish all the flaming
arrows of the evil one." (Ephesians 6:16)*

The next piece of armor to be employed in spiritual
battle is the "shield of faith." The Roman soldier
used a number of different shields in battle. One of
the more commonly used was a small, round shield that
was strapped to the soldier's forearm. The kind of shield
Paul is referring to here was called the *thureos*, which comes
from the Greek word for "door." Shaped like a door, the
shield was typically about 2' × 4', large enough to cover
most of the average-sized soldier's body. It was often made
of two layers of sturdy, laminated wood covered by a heavy
animal hide. A strip of iron on the top and bottom of the
shield held the material in place. The shields were often
soaked in water, which added to their weight and their ability to absorb the flaming arrows of the enemy.

The soldiers who carried these large shields were positioned in front of the marching army. They would stand

close enough so that their shields touched, making the troops impervious to the enemy's attacks. From the opposing army's position, the view was that of a solid wall moving steadily toward them. R. Kent Hughes notes that "very often the [enemy's arrow] would snuff out as it buried itself in the thickness of the shield. During battles these great shields would often bristle with smoking arrows like roasted porcupines."[13]

Every year, innovations are made in law enforcement equipment. One of these innovations in recent years has been the development of the ballistic shield. It's interesting that the ballistic shield used by today's peace officer is very similar in size and shape to the *thureos* carried by Roman soldiers 2,000 years ago. Like the *thureos*, the ballistic shield is designed to provide cover for the majority of the peace officer's body. There are different types of ballistic shields. Some are solid pieces of iron, but the more popular model is made of a Kevlar composite. It is a very effective tool during the execution of search warrants. I've used this shield a number of times for that very purpose.

Holding the Shield

On November 30, 2002, Los Angeles County Sheriff's Deputy David Powell and several other deputies assigned to Lakewood Station answered a "923" (shots fired) call. When they arrived at the location, the deputies were told that the gun-wielding suspect had entered a house and may be holding a woman hostage. Powell and another deputy made their way to a door at the back of the house where they could see the suspect moving about inside.

As the two deputies positioned themselves at the door, preparing to enter because they believed a woman's life was in danger, shots came through the door. One struck Deputy

Powell on an area of his upper body that was not covered by his vest. The deputy with Powell returned fire through the door, killing the suspect. Sadly, Deputy Powell died from his wound, joining the all-too-long list of brave men and women who have made the ultimate sacrifice protecting the citizens of our country.

Deputy Powell, a follower of Jesus Christ, was known as a hard-charging, conscientious street cop who could be counted on for backup by his fellow deputies in any situation. His dedication to working patrol was such that, following his death, Los Angeles County Sheriff Lee Baca instituted a new Department award, "The Legendary Lawman Award," bestowed upon any deputy who has worked a patrol assignment for ten or more years. Deputy Powell was the award's first recipient. Regrettably, he received it posthumously.

The ballistic shield used by today's peace officer is very similar in size and shape to the thureos carried by Roman soldiers 2,000 years ago.

Less than a day after Deputy Powell was murdered, I found myself with a group of deputies just blocks away from where Dave was killed. We were in a standoff with a man—reportedly with a gun—who was standing on his porch, holding his four-year-old daughter as a human shield. For the next hour, I held a ballistic shield and stood several yards from the man, as we tried to talk him into surrendering. Fortunately, the incident ended peacefully, with the child uninjured and the unarmed, agitated man taken into custody.

Looking back on that day, I remember standing on that sidewalk with my attention focused on an unstable, potentially armed man, who was willing to put a little girl in harm's way. Though I was paying very close attention to the suspect, the positions of my fellow deputies, and my own tactics, I also found myself praising God. In my heart and mind, I praised Him for allowing me to be a chaplain for the deputies who were with me on that street and for allowing me to serve alongside them in the trenches.

During that potentially dangerous call, I held the shield with a certain amount of faith—faith in the ability of the shield to do its job should the suspect have a gun and decide to shoot at me; faith in my fellow deputies to handle the call with sound tactics, common sense, and courage; and faith in the Lord to see me through this situation, as He has so faithfully done in every other circumstance.

One True Faith

The faith Paul is referring to when he speaks of carrying the spiritual "shield of faith" is a trust in God that comes only through faith in Jesus Christ. It's the kind of faith that believes God is sovereign because God says He is sovereign. "The LORD has established His throne in the heavens, and His sovereignty rules over all" (Psalm 113:19).

It's the kind of faith that believes the Word of God is true because the Word of God says it's true. "The sum of Your word is truth, and every one of Your righteous ordinances is everlasting" (Psalm 119:160).

It's the kind of faith that believes that Jesus Christ is the only way of salvation because Jesus said He is the only way. Jesus Himself said, "I am the way, and the truth, and the life; no one comes to the Father, but through Me" (John 14:6).

Although childlike in the most positive way, there's nothing childish about this kind of faith. There's nothing ignorant or blind about this kind of faith. John MacArthur explains that faith in Christ "is far from being simply 'faith in something.' Faith is only as reliable and helpful as the trustworthiness of its object; and Christian faith is powerful and effective because the object of faith, Jesus Christ, is infinitely powerful and absolutely dependable. Christian faith never fails, because the One in whom that faith is placed never fails."[14]

The Scriptures define faith this way: "Now faith is the assurance of things hoped for, the conviction of things not seen" (Hebrews 11:1). Faith is following Jesus Christ even when the road of this life and the outcome of any given circumstance is uncertain.

According to James Montgomery Boice, the shield of faith serves to do three things: "(1) it should cover us so that not a portion is exposed, (2) it should link up with the faith of others to [present] a solid wall of defense, and (3) because it covers our entire person and links up with the faith of our fellow soldiers, it should be able to strike down whatever fiery arrows the enemy hurls at us."[15]

Facing Fiery Arrows

So, what kind of fiery arrows or ammunition does Satan launch at us? If we consider that the purpose of firing arrows from long distance was to penetrate the frontline shields of the Roman soldiers—to knock down their line of defense—then we should look at Satan's fiery arrows as attempts to penetrate the frontlines of our faith. He does this by trying to entice us to forsake our trust in God, to succumb to temptations, and to doubt that God is able to handle anything that comes our way.

But, if we stand firm, if we hold our shields of faith in front of us, those fiery arrows will be extinguished. They will become little more than burnt and smoldering sticks that serve as reminders that the enemy is real and that a genuine faith in Christ will protect us and help us to win victory after victory over an already defeated foe.

Some Roman soldiers, perhaps those experiencing their first major battle, threw down their shields when they saw the arrows burning on the shield's surface. They dropped their shields and ran the other way, opening themselves up to a deadly arrow in the back. The same can happen to us. If instead of standing firm in our faith in Christ, we rely on our own wisdom and go off in a direction of our own choosing, we open ourselves up to temptation and sin, which will likely be painful, and sometimes even deadly.

I find it very interesting that Paul's description of spiritual armor doesn't mention any piece of armament that specifically protects the soldier's back. A soldier was at his greatest peril when he turned his back on his enemy.

Paul's description of spiritual armor doesn't mention any piece of armament that specifically protects the soldier's back.

The first of the reality television cop shows, entertaining audiences for more than a decade now, is "Cops." I used to be an avid viewer of the show but, over the years, I have found it just too difficult to watch sometimes. Although I am not one to armchair quarterback other peace officers' work in the field, there are times when the safety tactics of officers profiled on the show leave a great deal to be desired. I don't know how many times I have found myself yelling at the television—as if the officers inside the picture tube could actually hear me—for the officers to take better control of a suspect, or to not climb into a car to conduct a search while an unsecured suspect stands behind them, watching their every move.

Basic safety tactics dictate that officers never take their eyes off an unsecured suspect. You never turn your back on someone who has the potential to cause you harm. And when faced with a potentially violent confrontation, that is not the time to throw your weapons to the ground and run in the opposite direction. The same is true when we face the onslaught of our spiritual enemy, when Satan is firing flaming arrows of doubt and temptation our way. That is not the time to throw down your shield of faith.

To win the spiritual battles of this life, we must carry the shield of faith. However, Christians need not rely on their own strength to carry the shield. In fact, it would be foolish to do so.

Cicero, the Roman statesman and orator, once said, "A man of courage is also full of faith." Because God is faithful, the one who trusts in Him can be faithful. And because this is true, we can agree with the psalmist who writes, "The LORD preserves the faithful and fully recompenses the proud doer. Be strong and let your heart take courage, all you who hope in the LORD" (Psalm 31:23,24).

God has also told His people throughout the ages that it takes courage to live by faith. He imparted this wisdom to one of his greatest warriors, Joshua: "Have I not commanded you? Be strong and courageous! Do not tremble or be dismayed, for the LORD your God is with you wherever you go" (Joshua 1:9). Joshua could be strong and courageous because he believed by faith that the Lord would be with him wherever he went. And every follower of Jesus Christ can live by faith with the same assurance.

So, stand firm, holding tightly the shield of faith the Lord has given you. Do not tremble or be dismayed when attacks from your spiritual enemy come, regardless of the form they may take. The enemy wants you to drop your shield, to lose confidence in your faith in Christ. He wants you to turn your back on the Lord's provision and protection so that he can strike you down, wounding you with the arrows of temptation and despair. He wants you to rely on your own strength and your own wisdom. The enemy's best offense is to scare or frustrate the follower of Christ into relinquishing the impenetrable defensive position of trust in the Lord.

You are safe and secure so long as your heart remains steadfast in the Lord Jesus Christ. With such confident faith comes great promise. One such promise is this: "He will not fear evil tidings; his heart is steadfast, trusting in the LORD. His heart is upheld, he will not fear, until he looks with satisfaction on his adversaries" (Psalm 112:7,8).

Standing secure behind the shield of faith in Christ enables believers to look upon their spiritual enemy with satisfaction—knowing that nothing the enemy throws at them, whether by way of circumstance or the actions of other people, can separate them from the love of God. The fiery arrows of the evil one will be quickly extinguished, rendered harmless by the protective covering that only faith in Jesus Christ can provide. So, take up your shield! Stand by faith in the One who is truly faithful.

Chapter Eight

THE HELMET OF SALVATION

"And take up the helmet of salvation…"
(Ephesians 6:17a)

The next piece of armor—the last defensive item—in Paul's list is the "helmet of salvation." Roman soldiers wore one of two helmets. They wore either the leather model, known as the *galea*, or the steel model, known as the *cassis*. In his commentary, R. Kent Hughes describes the helmet this way: "The helmet had a band to protect the forehead and plates for the cheeks, and extended down in back to protect the neck. When the helmet was strapped in place, it exposed little besides the eyes, nose, and mouth. The metal helmets, due to their weight, were lined with sponge or felt. Virtually the only weapons [that] could penetrate a metal helmet were hammers or axes."[16] If any piece of equipment should give the wearer the sense that he is a soldier gearing up for battle, it is the helmet.

Peace officers have helmets, too. Cops commonly refer to them as "riot helmets." The name comes from the circumstances in which a peace officer is most likely to don a helmet. Like the *cassis*, the helmet I carry in my "war bag" is heavy, with an interior that is lined with several foam pads. My helmet also has a face shield to protect my eyes and most of my face.

Protecting one's head and face is vital to the peace officer. Injuries to the head, even if they are not serious, can be incapacitating. There are probably few things as frightening to the peace officer as the thought of passing out, due to a head injury, while fighting with a suspect. Even a momentary lapse in consciousness or clarity of mind during a violent confrontation can be fatal. So, a certain amount of defensive tactics training for law enforcement officers focuses attention on protecting the head and face.

We should be every bit as conscientious to protect our heads in the spiritual battles of life. Consider the words of Charles Spurgeon:

> Soldiers, look to your heads. A wound in the head is a serious matter. Since the head is a vital part, we need to well protect it. The heart needs to be guarded with the breastplate, but the head needs just as much protection, for even if man is true-hearted, if a shot should go through his brain, the body ends strewn on the plain. There are Christians who get their hearts warmed and think that is enough. Give me above everything else a good warm heart, but, oh to have that warm heart coupled with a head that is well taken care of. Do you know that a hot head and a hot heart together do a great deal of mischief, but with a hot heart and a cool head, you may do a world of service for the Master?
>
> Have right doctrine in the head, and then set the soul on fire, and you will soon win the world. There is [none] standing in the person's way whose head and

heart are both right, but many Christians have caused serious trouble by neglecting the head. They have been almost useless because they have not taken care of their brains. They arrive in heaven, but they have few victories because they have never been able to clearly understand the doctrine—they have not been able to give a reason for the hope that lies within them. They have not, in fact, looked well to the helmet that was to cover their heads.

The text refers us to our head because it speaks of a helmet, and a helmet is useful only to the head. Among other reasons that we should preserve the head in the day of battle, let us give these. The head is peculiarly liable to the temptations of Satan, of self, and of fame...The head [is] liable to attacks from skepticism...The head is very greatly in danger from attacks of personal unbelief...[And] some believers are attacked by threatenings from the world...But there is no danger to the man who has his helmet on.

No, let the arrows fly thick as hail, and let the foes have all political power and all the prestige of antiquity that they may. A little group of true-hearted Christians will stand out at the thick of the onslaught and cut their way to glory and victory through whole hosts because their heads are guarded with the heavenly helmet of the hope of salvation. Soldiers, then, take care of your heads.[17]

The L.A. Riots

While working in the jails early in my career, I made use of my riot helmet on several occasions. It was an important piece of safety equipment, used when I and other deputies were called upon to quell inmate uprisings in one of the county's jail facilities. Having dealt with a number of riots while working in the county jail, I can tell you that inmates have a tendency to have second thoughts about taking on the deputies once they see the troops moving toward them. When the Emergency Response Team would arrive in full riot gear (including helmets), the inmates knew that the deputies were serious and weren't there to socialize.

As I reflect on the times when my riot helmet was both necessary and useful, the most significant incident that comes to mind occurred during the first several days of May 1992. Throughout the country, the incident is now commonly referred to as the "Los Angeles Riots."

Having spent the first several years of my career working in custody division, I was still relatively new to patrol. In fact, the first day of the riots was my first day off patrol training—a six-month period in which deputies are tested and evaluated to determine if they belong on the streets. I remember gathering with other deputies in the station's briefing room. The room was packed. We huddled around a television to watch as the verdict was read in the trial of four Los Angeles police officers. The officers stood accused of using excessive force against a criminal by the name of Rodney King. At the time, the news media referred to King merely as a "motorist." Those of us in the law enforcement family disagreed with that title.

You could feel the tension in the room build as the foreman of the jury began to read the verdicts. When we learned that all four officers had been acquitted of all charges, we felt a sense of relief. We all realized that, on any given day, circumstances could be such that each of us could find ourselves in a similar situation. We were relieved for the officers. We were relieved for their families. We were relieved for our brothers and sisters in blue—the LAPD. But, the tension we felt as we awaited the verdict was quickly replaced with a new tension as we awaited the inevitable backlash in the communities of Los Angeles County.

We didn't have to wait very long.

Soon after I arrived at home, Mahria and I found ourselves glued to the television as the situation began to unfold in the middle of a now-famous intersection in the southern part of Los Angeles. We watched in horror as common street thugs, with uncommon ferocity, attacked unsuspecting motorists (and these people could rightly be referred to as "motorists"). I could feel the anger well up inside me as I watched these barbarians pull driver Reginald Denny from his truck, drag him to the ground, beat and kick him, and jubilantly crush his skull with a brick.

When the Emergency Response Team would arrive in full riot gear, the inmates knew that the deputies weren't there to socialize.

I turned my attention to Mahria. The look on her face told me that her worry extended beyond Reginald Denny and the other innocent people being victimized by criminal opportunists (not civic-minded citizens upset with what they believed to be an unjust verdict). Her concern was for me and for what I would likely be called to do. I looked at her and said, "I'm probably going to go down there." It wasn't long before the call came.

The next morning I reported to Santa Clarita Valley Station and, with a platoon of deputies, made my way into the heart of Los Angeles—a city whose devastation was already evident. It was an eerie feeling as I sat in one of a dozen radio cars rolling "Code-3" down the freeway. We were the only cars on the road heading into the city. The only civilian traffic was the result of people making their way out of a city under siege. As we got closer to the city, it looked like a war zone. Buildings were either ablaze or smoldering. Many of the structures were just heaps of rubble. It looked like the city had been bombed.

Once our platoon reported to one of the many command posts in the city, we were deployed to provide perimeter security for the area surrounding a major shopping mall. With my helmet on and baton in hand, I stood with several other deputies, blocking a street from all unauthorized traffic. As we manned our post, several people drove up to us, jumped out of their cars, and re-enacted the now-famous Rodney King videotape. They simulated baton strikes upon one of their cohorts, who was lying on the ground and playing the role of Rodney King. They yelled profanities and tried to taunt us into a confrontation. During these antagonistic melodramas, it was not uncommon for a glass bottle or other projectile to crash at our feet, having been thrown by an assailant hidden inside, atop, or behind a nearby building. I was glad to have my helmet.

Speaking from experience, the riot helmet has a psychological impact on both the wearer and the people facing the wearer. If you ever find yourself standing in front of peace officers, in formation, wearing riot gear, and you aren't at least a little apprehensive, you might want to check your ability to perceive possible danger. From the opposite perspective, there is a certain confidence and peace that comes to officers when they don the riot helmet. Putting on the helmet not only reminds peace officers that the situation is serious and potentially dangerous, but it also reminds them of their training and experience, the rightness of what they are about to do, the honor that comes with serving in situations from which most people flee, and the knowledge that they are not alone. There are fellow peace officers on either side, ready to provide backup and to ensure everyone gets through the situation alive.

A Confident Hope

The apostle Paul tells believers, "Let us be sober, having put on...as a helmet, the hope of salvation" (1 Thessalonians 5:8). That's what he has in mind in the verse we're looking at—the hope of salvation. It's not the hope of being saved one day. Remember, Paul is writing to people who have already received the free gift of eternal life through Jesus Christ. Paul is looking to a future hope—a future hope of the realization of the believer's salvation. It's hope in the assurance that one day we will enjoy the rest, peace, joy, and perfect fellowship with our Lord and continual unfettered, unabashed worship of Him, in heaven for all eternity.

If we are wearing the "helmet of salvation"—the helmet that reminds us of the precious gift we have already received and the perfect fulfillment of that gift we will one day enjoy—then we should exude confidence, even in the midst of battle with the enemy. Again, it's not confidence in ourselves. It's not confidence that comes from relying on our own strength and wisdom. Remember that this is the armor of *God*, and that He is the source of our strength: "O GOD the Lord, the strength of my salvation, You have covered my head in the day of battle" (Psalm 140:7).

Our confidence is in Christ and the assurance of everything He has promised to those who truly love and obey Him—a confidence that prepares us not simply to dig in our heels and wait to be attacked, but to stand firm, knowing that the enemy cannot harm us and our future is secure.

Satan will surely try to attack our confidence in Christ when he wages war in our lives. Don't let him. Put on the "helmet of salvation," and let it serve as a reminder that the battle you are fighting is a battle against an enemy who has already been defeated by our sovereign Lord, Jesus Christ.

As I shared in my personal testimony at the beginning of this book, my eternal hope is in none other than Jesus Christ—my Lord and my Savior. It is because of my hope in Christ—my confident assurance that He has saved me from my sin and that I will one day enjoy the full benefit of my salvation with Him in heaven—that I can paraphrase the following passage of Scripture and apply it directly to my life.

> For [I was] once foolish [myself], disobedient, deceived, enslaved to various lusts and pleasures, spending [my] life in malice and envy, hateful, hating [others]. But when the kindness of God [my] Savior and His love for mankind appeared, He saved [me], not on the basis of deeds which [I] had done in righteousness, but according to His mercy, by the washing of regeneration and renewing by the Holy Spirit, whom He poured out upon [me] richly through Jesus Christ [my] Savior, so that being justified by His grace [I] would be made [an heir] according to the hope of eternal life. (Titus 3:3–7, paraphrased)

Do You Share My Hope?

Do you share the hope that I have in Jesus Christ? Are you standing firm on the spiritual battlefield knowing that the helmet of salvation—a piece of armor that the Lord has graciously given to those who believe—provides you with the necessary protection when the enemy attacks?

If you are putting your hope in yourself or in the world, then you're going to get hurt. And if you don't know Jesus Christ as your Lord and Savior, the wounds (caused by your own sin), no matter how slight, *will* be mortal, resulting in an eternal existence in hell. But if your hope is in Christ alone, then the helmet of salvation will protect you from any and all mortal wounds.

Sure, you may take a hit or two. You may be battered and bruised from time to time. You may walk away from a spiritual fight with a bit of a spiritual headache. But if you are wearing the helmet of salvation because your hope and confidence in Christ is genuine, then the spiritual wounds will not be mortal. Your sins are forgiven, and nothing can separate you from the one-day, fully realized hope of eternity with the Lord. We can cling to this wonderful promise of Scripture:

> For I am convinced that neither death, nor life, nor angels, nor principalities, nor things present, nor things to come, nor powers, nor height, nor depth, nor any other created thing, will be able to separate us from the love of God, which is in Christ Jesus our Lord. (Romans 8:38,39)

Chapter Nine

THE SWORD
OF THE SPIRIT

*"... and the sword of the Spirit, which is the
word of God." (Ephesians 6:17b)*

Last, but not least, Paul mentions the only offensive
weapon in his list of spiritual warfare armament. It's
the "sword of the Spirit, which is the word of God."
Remember that much of the fighting done by Roman soldiers involved hand-to-hand combat. The weapons of the
day were designed, by and large, with this in mind. The
sword most often used by Roman foot soldiers was no
exception.

The sword preferred by the Roman soldier was the
machaira, which was anywhere from six to eighteen inches
in length. John MacArthur describes this sword: "Carried in
a sheath or scabbard attached to [the soldiers'] belts, it was
always at hand and ready for use. It was the sword carried
by the soldiers who came to arrest Jesus in the Garden
(Matt. 26:47), wielded by Peter when he cut off the ear of
the high priest's slave (v. 51), and used by Herod's execu-
tioners to put [the apostle] James to death (Acts 12:2)."[18]

My Duty Weapon

The "sword" that I carry on duty is a Beretta 92F, 9mm, semi-automatic pistol, with a 15-round magazine and one round in the chamber. It is a far better weapon than the six-shot, Smith & Wesson, .38-caliber revolver I carried when I first joined the department. The ammunition I carry, as a deputy sheriff for L.A. County, is a 147 grain, jacketed, hollow-point round. The round is designed to penetrate well. It is also designed to spread, flatten, and slow as it enters the body. The reason this is important is that it provides the best stopping power for a round its size, and it's more likely to remain in a person's body once it enters. This provides some protection for innocent bystanders who might be near the person being hit with the round. Like the *machaira*, the Beretta is best used in close quarters. Statistics show that most police shootings occur within a distance of three feet and are over in about six seconds.

I've employed my service weapon while on duty, drawing it from its holster more times than I could ever count and firing it on one occasion. Weapons like the one I carry are of little use, and can be very dangerous—even deadly—if used by someone who is not properly trained. And they certainly can be deadly when used by a person with evil intentions. It's been said by opponents of tighter gun control, "Guns don't kill. People do."

Firearm Qualification and Proper Use

Like all peace officers around the country, deputies with the Los Angeles County Sheriff's Department are required to regularly qualify with their duty weapons. They have to show a certain level of proficiency before they are permitted not only to carry a weapon on duty, but to work in any capacity as a peace officer. They have to show that they can rightly handle a firearm and have a working knowledge of their department's policies regarding the use of firearms. Just because officers know how to use a firearm doesn't mean they can use it whenever and however they want, in any or all circumstances.

Likewise, we must be careful to rightly handle the Word of God. We must wield the sword in the manner in which it was intended—not in any fashion we choose.

There are those in certain religious circles today who will try to teach you that *your* words are powerful, that *your* words are a creative force that can speak things such as health, wealth, and prosperity into existence. They will also tell you that *your* words can cause Satan to tuck his tail between his legs and run away, yelping like a spanked puppy.

James Montgomery Boice hits the nail on the head when he writes, "Satan will not flee from us simply because we tell him to. He will retreat only before the power of God as [God] himself speaks his words into the midst of the temptation."[19] God has spoken His words through the Scriptures. If we are carrying the "sword of the Spirit," He will bring the appropriate and necessary Scriptures to our mind when temptation comes. But He will do this only if we are taking the time to read, study, mediate upon, and memorize His Word.

Furthermore, we need to make sure that we employ the Word of God in compliance with God's policies—within the confines of His sovereign will. What does that mean? It means that we need to be careful never to take God's Word out of context just so that we can win an argument, defend a sinful position, or chastise someone unmercifully for no reason other than to hurt that person.

The Bible tells us that God's Word is sharp enough on its own: "For the word of God is living and active and sharper than any two-edged sword, and piercing as far as the division of soul and spirit, of both joints and marrow, and able to judge the thoughts and intentions of the heart" (Hebrews 4:12). We shouldn't dip the tip of this powerful and effective sword in the poison of sinful intentions, thinking that doing so will in some way make it more effective. The mighty sword that is the very Word of God should only be used in such a way that it brings truth to the hearer.

The Bible tells us that "the word of the cross is foolishness to those who are perishing, but to us who are being saved it is the power of God" (1 Corinthians 1:18). I never worry about God's Word—on its own merits—being offensive. I expect it to be from time to time, especially among non-Christians. And I even expect it to be offensive to believers who insist on wallowing in their own sin. It may seem a bit cold, but my response is, "Oh, well." With that said, let me say that the cause of the offense should never be my sinful motives, wrong attitudes, or misapplication of God's Word. I should never use God's Word, the sword of the Spirit, in the wrong way.

Lieutenant Devin Chase of the Torrance Police Department, and President of Peace Officers for Christ, International, told me the following story.

> I answered a "459-Silent Alarm" call at a warehouse. As I walked up to a loading dock door on the side of the building, a man emerged from a hole in the loading dock. My gun, of course, was already out of its holster. I pointed it at the suspect and ordered him to "freeze."

> As a rookie cop, I think I put too much stock in the power of my gun. So, I expected my actions of point-

ing a loaded gun at a bad guy to work just like I had been told. The bad guy was supposed to put his hands up and move to a prone position on the ground. Once he complied, I would safely approach him, slap hand-cuffs on his wrists, and make my first solo felony arrest.

Unfortunately, the suspect knew department policy and state law at least as well as I did. Instead of com-plying with my commands, he simply raised his hands in the air and, in a very calm voice, said, "Officer, you can see my hands. And you can see that I don't have any weapons, right?"

Of course, in my confused rookie mind, I an-swered, "Yes."

With the same calm voice, the burglar said, "Then you can't shoot me." He then turned and ran away. I realized that I was now carrying a 5-pound "Smith & Wesson" paperweight as I went in foot pursuit of the burglar. I couldn't use my weapon outside of policy.

Sadly, unlike Lieutenant Chase, some peace officers over the years have used their firearms inappropriately. Peace officers who use their firearms outside of policy, whether or not someone is injured or killed, will face disciplinary ac-tion, at the very least, and even termination. The same is true for Christians who wrongfully employ God's Word. Take God's Word out of context, use His Word for sinful and illicit personal gain (as we see so often nowadays among televangelists), or use it to put people down instead of build them up and point them to Christ, then don't be surprised if you experience God's discipline somewhere along the way. And don't be surprised if the misuse of God's Word one day leads to your disqualification, in one way or anoth-er, from using it in the future.

How quick will others be to listen to something you say about God if you have misused God's Word and misled them in the past? When I served as a field training officer, I was tasked not only with knowing department policy and procedures, but also with making sure my trainees knew them. I also had to ensure that my trainees knew how to *apply* those policies and procedures. If I were ever to give one of my trainees wrong information, or if I misinterpreted policies and procedures, leading him or her to face discipline (or worse, injury), then I should not be surprised if that trainee became hesitant to take my advice and counsel in the future. Likewise, how many true students of the Word would stay under your teaching if they couldn't trust you to rightly divide the Word of God for them because you had failed to do so in the past?

Again, if our behavior or the manner in which we present the truths of God's Word to others is inconsistent with scriptural teaching, that's sinful. Probably the best biblical example of this is found in the account of Satan's overt and futile attempts to entice Jesus to sin (Matthew 4:1–11). Satan repeatedly took the Word of God out of context as he tried to tempt Jesus. But Satan was easily defeated when Jesus countered his attack with the *truth* of His Word, rightly divided and rightly applied.

Again, if we misuse the Word of God, it is sin; if God's Word is offensive to unbelievers, it is biblical. The Bible gives us several examples of this during Jesus' earthly ministry, such as when He took the Jewish leaders to task because they "invalidated the word of God for the sake of [their] tradition." He told them:

> "You hypocrites, rightly did Isaiah prophesy of you:
> 'This people honors Me with their lips, but their heart

is far away from Me. But in vain do they worship Me, teaching as doctrines the precepts of men.'"... Then the disciples came and said to Him, "Do You know that the Pharisees were offended when they heard this statement?" (Matthew 15:7–9,12)

Jesus, who knew no sin, offended the religious leaders of His day when He *rightly* used the Word of God to expose their hypocrisy and sin. Knowing that the Word of God is an offensive weapon should not cause us to hesitate to pull the sword from its sheath. Jesus never hesitated to do so. As His disciples, Christians just need to be sure to use the "sword of the Spirit" in the right way.

Don't Be Afraid to Offend

I remember working patrol one night when my partner and I were checking turnouts on a remote canyon road. Turnouts such as these were good places to make arrests for drug use and other nefarious activities. Sometimes we would get lucky and make a good hook. More often than not we would find couples looking for places to be alone.

As we often did, this night we came upon a man and a woman sitting in a car. We bathed the vehicle and its occupants with our headlights, spotlights, and flashlights. As I approached the driver's door, I asked to see the driver's hands, which were not on the steering wheel but were somewhere below the door window, out of sight. I knew that the man's eyes couldn't kill me. I knew that his mouth couldn't kill me. But his hands—well, they most certainly could kill me. The man refused to show me his hands.

With a little more force behind my voice, I again ordered the man to show me his hands. He looked at me and sarcastically said, "What for?" The third time I asked I did so with the barrel of my gun pointed at his nose. His hands were now in the air, but he wasn't happy. "Do I look like a criminal to you?" he asked. "You can't point your gun at me!"

Long story made short, after separating the man from his vehicle and curtly explaining to him how close he came to getting hurt, we dusted him off and sent him and his girlfriend on their way. The man was upset with us, but I think his girlfriend was more upset with him. I don't think the night turned out as he planned.

The third time I asked I did so with the barrel of my gun pointed at his nose. His hands were now in the air, but he wasn't happy.

We dropped by the station later on that night. The watch commander saw us and called us into his office. The man at whom I pointed my gun had called to file a complaint. He was offended that I pointed my gun at him. Once I explained the circumstances to the watch commander, he called the man at home and explained to him that in the future, if a deputy sheriff orders him to show his hands, common sense and personal safety should dictate that he comply.

Now, more than ever, people seem to be easily offended by peace officers who take appropriate and sometimes forceful police action. The most dangerous thing officers can do is worry more about a possible complaint than about maintaining their safety. Hesitation can kill a peace officer. The actions I took that night on that dark canyon road were right, based on my training, experiences, and the circumstances. The wrong decision would have been to not pull my weapon for fear I would have offended the man in the car.

My personal policy, one that I've stressed to the newly assigned patrol deputies I've had the opportunity to train, is that if I'm faced with a situation where the right decision is to exert my authority or use physical force, then I will do so without hesitation. I will worry about the ramifications for my decision later. It's more important for me to run the risk of facing a complaint than to have someone from the department knock on my door and tell Mahria I won't be coming home because I didn't act when I should have.

Many times I have heard Christians say that they are hesitant to share their faith, to take the sword of the Spirit out of its sheath, because they don't want to offend anyone. They don't want to come across as judgmental or as a "Bible thumper." Or, they question and worry about whether the Scriptures are relevant to the person to whom they are speaking. So they say nothing and miss an opportunity to share the life-saving gospel with someone who needs to hear it.

Again, let me quote R. Kent Hughes: "Face the truth—we are at war, and our razor-sharp weapon is God's Word, and we are fools to keep it in the scabbard simply because our culture says it cannot cut. That is what the enemy wants us to believe, that it is 'irrelevant,' and 'archaic' and 'not understandable,' so keep it in the sheath, where it is, of course, harmless."[20]

Confidence in Your Weapon

Keep this in mind, too. When Satan attacks by trying to entice us to sin, when our own flesh—which assails us more often than Satan does—attacks by tempting us to sin, it's time not only to defend ourselves, but also to take the offensive against the schemes of the devil. And the weapon we are called to use, by God's Word, is God's Word. As Jesus' encounter with Satan shows, the true and proper use of the "sword of the Spirit" is to counter the attacks of the enemy.

Not only are we called to rightly use the Word of God, but also we must fully and completely trust in the rightness of the Word of God. Theologian B. B. Warfield once said, "Nor do we need to do more than remind ourselves that this attitude of entire trust in every word of the Scriptures has been characteristic of the people of God from the very foundation of the church."[21]

A peace officer wouldn't think of working the streets with a weapon that he did not trust to work whenever it was needed. It is sickening, even horrifying, to the officer to think of finding himself in a situation where the use of deadly force is warranted, and yet he cannot respond due to a defective weapon. Part of weapons training in law enforcement includes becoming proficient in correcting weapon malfunctions during stressful situations, in order to avoid such a tragedy.

I was involved in a shooting on February 6, 1993. Another deputy and I were forced to fire upon a grand theft auto suspect who was high on methamphetamine and tried to run us over with a stolen car. Neither I nor the other deputy was injured. The suspect was taken into custody and was later sentenced to 11 years in state prison for two counts of attempted murder on a peace officer.

Prior to that fateful day, I frequently experienced a recurring dream—a nightmare, really. In the dream I found myself in a darkened alley, alone with a suspect. The suspect's appearance could best be described as demonic. The only features of the suspect I could make out were a fiendish grin and bright yellow eyes. As the suspect made his way toward me, I drew my weapon and ordered him to stop. Every time I did this, the suspect would laugh and lunge toward me. Believing that my life was in danger, I pulled the trigger of my weapon, but nothing happened. The gun didn't work! After several attempts, the gun finally discharged a round, but the bullet simply fell out of the barrel, landing on the ground at my feet. The suspect's laugh grew louder and more insidious. Just as the suspect was about to grab hold of me, I would wake up, often sweating.

Interestingly enough, since the day I was involved in the real-life shooting, I've never again had that dream or any dream like it. It's as if the shooting reaffirmed in my heart and mind that not only would my gun work if I ever needed to use it, but that I would have the wherewithal to take whatever action was necessary to protect myself, my partners, or someone in the community. I would pull the trigger if I had to.

Just as the peace officer must trust in the reliability and functionality of his weapon, so, too, the Christian must trust in the infallibility and inerrancy of God's Word. Peace officers will not use weapons that they don't believe will work. Likewise, Christians will be hesitant to turn to Scripture in times of doubt and temptation or to share the gospel if they do not fully trust that the Word of God is true, powerful, and effective. We need only look to the Scriptures themselves to receive all the evidence we need that God's Word is trustworthy. The Bible assures us: "All Scripture is inspired by God and profitable for teaching, for reproof, for correction, for training in righteousness; so that the man of God may be adequate, equipped for every good work" (2 Timothy 3:16,17).

Keep Training

Do you want to stand firm against the schemes of the devil? Do you want to be able to withstand your own sinful desires? Do you want to be fully equipped, ready, and confident to use the weapon God has provided? Then get your sword, the Word of God, out of its sheath! Get your Bible out more often than on Sunday morning. Train with it every day. Meditate on it (think about it) every day. Learn the truth it contains. Apply the truth it contains. Live the truth it contains. Stand firm on the truth of God's Word, which is given to us from the very breath of God as He inspired the Bible's writers.

Peace officers train regularly with their duty weapons, and the training extends beyond simply hitting a target when they pull the trigger. They train to quickly remove their weapons from their holsters. As Christians, we should spend so much time in the Word that it becomes natural for us to impart Scripture into our day-to-day conversations.

If a man dresses up like a cop and walks down the street, people might look at him and think he is a cop. But that doesn't make him a peace officer.

Peace officers train to clear jams and correct malfunctions during stressful situations. As Christians, we should be so familiar with the Word that it is the first thing to come to mind during times of stress, doubt, and temptation.

Peace officers train to keep suspects from taking their weapons, and they train to take weapons away from assailants if they find themselves being held at gunpoint. As Christians, we should study the Word so that we are able to immediately recognize when Scripture is being misinterpreted and misapplied, and so that we are equipped in the discipline of safeguarding the Word from those who would seek to distort or deny the truth it contains.

Like the peace officer who is trained and ready to use his or her firearm, may you carry "the sword of the Spirit, which is the word of God," always ready to use it rightly in whatever spiritual battles you face.

Impersonating an Officer

There you have it—the believer's armor, the uniform of "God's peace officer." Are you wearing it? If so, your armament will enable you to withstand every attack of your spiritual enemy. With the armor of God to protect you, you will be able to walk through the battleground of this earthly kingdom to arrive safely one day in God's eternal kingdom. While the enemy can tempt and taunt you, you need not surrender! You have everything you need to be victorious, for now and for eternity.

However, perhaps as you are reading this, it all seems very new or even foreign to you. There's something you need to know. If a man wakes up one morning and decides he is going to go out and buy a police uniform and the accompanying equipment, and he dresses up like a cop and walks down the street, people might look at him and *think* he is a cop. But that doesn't make him a peace officer. He is only impersonating an officer, which is a crime.

To be a peace officer, an individual must go through an extensive background investigation, be hired by a law enforcement agency, swear an oath to uphold the laws of the state and the Constitution of our nation, survive an academy, and successfully complete field training. Only after this does the person have the right to wear the badge and uniform and legitimately use the various pieces of equipment we've looked at. The same is true when it comes to wearing the spiritual armor Paul talks about in Ephesians 6. Only the genuine believer in Jesus Christ—only the person who has received the free gift of salvation that comes through repentance and faith—can rightly wear the spiritual armor of the believer.

Without Christ as your Lord and Savior, you can pretend to put on the belt of truth, the breastplate of righteousness, the shoes fitted with the readiness of the gospel of peace, the shield of faith, the helmet of salvation, and the sword of the Spirit, but it will be nothing more than a fancy suit of clothes. Not only that, but you will have no idea how to use the various pieces for God's glory and for your own defense against the enemy. You might be able to convince other people that the clothes fit you, but God will know that you simply pulled them off the rack and that it's nothing more than an impersonation. It doesn't have to be that way.

Whether you are legitimately wearing the spiritual armor of the believer will affect not just your time on earth, but also your future in eternity. You will need to have on the armor of God when you stand in His eternal courtroom one day. If you have not been properly attired by God, if He has not custom tailored this uniform for you, then the following pages are for you. Please read them carefully.

Chapter Ten

YOUR DAY
IN COURT

I'm often asked about how I'm able to balance serving as both a reserve deputy sheriff and a chaplain. I usually begin my answer by saying, "I wear two hats." I go on to explain that whenever I'm working as a deputy, I'm also serving as a chaplain. And whenever I'm called upon to serve as a chaplain, I do so as a deputy sheriff—a member of the law enforcement family.

When asked this question, I often share the story of the day when I detained a man for possession of a small amount of marijuana. As I handcuffed him, he noticed the crosses on my uniform collar. He lifted his chin, as if to point with his head toward my collar, and asked, "What are those?" I told him that not only was I a deputy sheriff, but I also serve the deputies as their chaplain.

A smile grew on the man's face. I could tell that even through his marijuana-fogged mind he was formulating a plan to get out of the trouble in which he presently found himself. The man looked at me, looked at my collar, then looked back at me and said, "So, you're going to forgive me, right?"

The man thought that since the station chaplain was detaining him, benevolence would win the day and I would give him a break—let him go. It was now my turn to smile. I looked the man in the eye while placing my Smith & Wesson chrome bracelets on his wrists and, with the most sympathetic voice I could muster, said, "Oh, I forgive you. These are just the consequences for your actions." The smile disappeared from his face as I put him in the backseat of my patrol car.

Wearing two hats at the same time can be a challenge— a challenge to properly balance the heart and mind of a street cop with the heart and mind of a chaplain. It is only by God's grace and the indwelling of His Holy Spirit that I can even come close to hitting the mark. But with this day-to-day challenge has come wonderful opportunities to serve the Lord while serving as a deputy sheriff. I would like to share such an opportunity with you—one with which I was blessed just recently.

Accountable for the Crime

The call came out as a "traffic collision, no injuries—possible drunk driver." Our station area was experiencing the highest rainfall totals in almost a decade, and this day was wet.

My partner and I drove to the area of the call and found a damaged Honda Civic parked with the rear tires in someone's front lawn and the two flattened front tires in the street. As we got closer to the car, we could see the silhouettes of two people through the fogged windows.

We got out of our patrol car. I approached the driver's door, and my partner approached on the passenger side. The driver (nineteen years old) opened his door and stepped out. I immediately smelled the odor of marijuana on his breath and person. I asked the driver if he had been smoking marijuana. He said, "Oh, I love the weed!"

I searched the driver and placed him in the backseat of our patrol car. I returned to the damaged vehicle as my partner was instructing the seventeen-year-old passenger to get out of the car. As the passenger stood up, I could see a $10 bag of cocaine on his seat. Needless to say, we detained the kid for felony possession of cocaine.

During a search of the vehicle, I also found a small amount of morphine and a couple items of drug paraphernalia. The driver, too intoxicated to safely operate a vehicle, was eventually booked on two counts of drug possession, possession of drug paraphernalia, drunk driving, and furnishing illegal drugs to a minor. His passenger was booked for possession of cocaine. Eventually, both of them admitted to purchasing the cocaine from a known drug dealer, not far from where we found them.

We transported the two to the station. While en route to the station, I learned that the juvenile was nine months younger than my eldest daughter, Michelle. I also learned that his dad and step-dad are both peace officers. The children of peace officers are far from immune to problems with drugs and brushes with the law.

In keeping with our department's policy regarding the handling of juveniles, we contacted the kid's mother and asked her to come to the station. Since he had no prior criminal history, and since the felony for which he was detained was not a violent crime, he would be released to his mother after the booking process was complete.

Mad at God

When the mother arrived, I walked up to the front desk and introduced myself. I didn't recognize her. But she recognized me. She said she had visited a local church on a Sunday morning on which I had preached. *Okay, time to wear both hats,* I thought. She shared her sad personal story with me. She was disillusioned—emotionally and spiritually drained. The day's events involving her son certainly did nothing to help. She told me that she believed her son was mad at God.

I walked back to the report writing room, where we hold juveniles who meet the department's non-secure detention guidelines. I sat down to tackle the mound of paperwork that lay in front of me—the aspect of police work you don't see on most TV police dramas. After a few minutes, I looked up from my report at the young man sitting at the other end of the table, and said, "Your mom tells me that she thinks you're mad at God."

The look on his face told me he was surprised to have a deputy sheriff ask him such a question. "I don't know if I'm mad at God," he said. "I just don't think I believe in Him. After all that's happened in my life, I don't think He exists."

He went on to tell me that although he doesn't believe in God, he believes in faith and in karma. I explained to him that one's faith is only as reliable as the object of that faith. I pointed to a chair in the room and said, "If I put my faith in that chair, what good will that do me?" The young man agreed that it would be silly to put my faith in a chair. I told him that if he put his faith in people, regardless of who they are, they would eventually let him down. And if he put his faith in himself, the events of the day should be all the proof he needs that he would let himself down, too. He couldn't argue with that.

I explained to him that he was being booked for possession of cocaine, not because of the mistakes other people in his life had made, but because of the choices he had made.

It wasn't God's fault that he got arrested. He found himself in his present circumstances because of his own sin. If he wanted to blame someone, all he had to do was look in the mirror. To him, that was a sobering thought.

I let him stew on that for a while and went back to my reports. As I wrote, I thought that the courtroom analogy I have used so many times while sharing my faith would be perfect in this situation.[22] Who better to share it with than a young man who soon would stand before a judge to be held accountable for his crime?

When the booking process was complete, I walked the young man to the front lobby to release him into his mother's custody. I had his mother sign a citation, which indicated she promised to appear in court with her son. Her eyes were still red from crying.

The Courtroom Analogy

I told the young man that I wanted to tell him an analogy that I thought he could relate to. I reminded him that he would be standing before a juvenile court judge in sixty days. Here's what I shared with him:

"Let's say that from now until your court date you do everything right. You stop smoking and using drugs. You do well in school. You stop hanging out with knuckleheads who could care less about you. And you obey your mom. It's now your day in court and you are standing before the judge. You tell the judge that you're sorry for what you've done and that it will never happen again. You explain to the judge how 'good' you've been since the day you were arrested and that you hope he will take all of this into account before handing down his sentence. As you await his decision, you think to yourself that the judge looks like a fair guy. You're confident that he will do the right thing.

"The judge looks down at you from his bench and says, 'Son, I appreciate all the positive things you have done since the day of your arrest. But, being a righteous judge, I must hold you accountable for your crime. I am sentencing you to either a $100,000 fine or life in prison.'"

I could see the young man's eyes redden and fill with tears. His mother stood very quiet off to the side, repeatedly glancing at her son and then at me. I let the young man ponder the judge's decision for a few moments.

I asked the young man, "Considering what kind of day you've had, this story is probably hitting you close to home. Isn't it?" He nodded his head. Then I continued the analogy:

Like most, if not all, peace officers, I become frustrated when I see a judge show what I consider to be too much leniency.

"You tell the judge that such a harsh sentence doesn't seem fair. You argue that you're only seventeen and you don't have $100,000. You ask the judge to give you a break. The judge looks at you and says that because he is just, he must ensure that justice is served and that every criminal is punished. He must give you the penalty prescribed by law. The judge says, 'Since you can't pay the fine, I must sentence you to life in prison.'

"Just then a man walks into the courtroom—a man you don't know and have never seen before. He walks directly to the judge's bench and sets down $100,000 cash in front of him. The man points to you and says, 'I'm paying his fine. Please release him.'

"The judge looks at the money now on his bench, looks at you, and says, 'Your debt has been paid in full. You are free to go.'"

I asked the young man, "Wouldn't that be good news?" He again nodded his head.

I then explained that Jesus Christ, God in the flesh, came to earth, died on the cross, and rose from the dead to pay the full penalty for his sins. I spent the next several minutes sharing the gospel with him and his mother, grateful for the opportunity I had to wear two hats.

Accused of a Crime

As I reflect on that occasion, I'm reminded of the hundreds of times I have been in courtrooms. More often than not, the reason for my presence in court has been to testify against a suspected criminal or to sit with the prosecutor as the investigating officer. My attitude in court over the years has been consistent—an attitude one would expect from a peace officer. I want to win every case. I want justice to be served. I want bad guys to be held accountable for their actions.

Like most, if not all, peace officers, I become frustrated when I see a judge show what I consider to be too much leniency to someone who is guilty beyond a reasonable doubt. I become frustrated when the entrance to the courtroom resembles a revolving door where criminals enter and exit without receiving what I believe to be the just penalty for their crimes. I've talked to officers who have allowed this kind of frustration to turn into disillusionment, which in turn causes them to stop working as hard as they once did to take criminals off the streets.

Whether or not you are a peace officer, you may share my frustration. Do you think that there are times when the court system lets us down and fails to hold criminals accountable for their crimes? Let me also ask you this: Do you hold yourself to the same standard?

A very real fear among peace officers, even those who exemplify integrity, is the idea of finding themselves seated at the defense table instead of next to the prosecutor. The thought of making a mistake in the line of duty that rises to the level of criminal misconduct or exposes one to civil litigation, the thought of being found guilty of a crime or liable for damages done to another, is frightening.

As a result of my actions as a peace officer, I have been a named defendant in a number of civil lawsuits. By God's grace, the judge has either dismissed each case, or a jury has made a determination that my fellow deputies and I did nothing wrong. Even so, going through the depositions, hearings, and court trials is stressful. Each time, I've walked away from such a situation saying to myself, "I never want to go through that again."

Like my brothers and sisters behind the badge, I understand that we are living and working in a "sue-happy," litigious society. I have to constantly balance the need to be decisive in taking positive law enforcement action with the knowledge that I must be aware of the possible ramifications for every action I take. I understand that my actions —accidental or intentional—can place me before a judge in court. It's a sobering thought.

I can imagine that many of you reading this may be nodding your heads in agreement. So, let me ask you this: How much thought have you given to the fact that one day you will stand before the Supreme Judge of the universe, the Creator of all things, Almighty God? The Bible is clear: "It is appointed for men to die once and after this comes judgment" (Hebrews 9:27).

How do you think you will do on that day? Just as there are civil laws that apply to all of society, there is a universal Moral Law by which we are to abide. You don't want to go through life thinking you're doing the right thing only to face the frightening prospect of finding yourself before the judge and declared guilty of breaking the Law. So, please take a few moments to look with me at God's Law, the Ten Commandments, to see how you will fare on that day.

The Standard of Judgment

One of the Ten Commandments says that we shouldn't lie. Have you ever told a lie? If you have, what does that make you? (Someone who lies is called a liar.) Another one of the Commandments says that we shouldn't steal. Have you ever stolen anything, no matter how small or insignificant the item might have been? If so, you are a thief. Have you ever looked at someone with lust? The Seventh Commandment says that we should not commit adultery. But Jesus said that looking lustfully at someone other than your spouse is the same as committing adultery with that person in your heart.

How are you doing so far? If you've broken these three Laws, you've admitted to being a lying, thieving, adulterer at heart. And that's only three of the Ten Commandments. Let's look at a couple more.

Most of us can say that we've never committed murder, but Jesus said that if you even hate someone you are a murderer. According to God's standard, have you broken this Commandment? Have you ever taken God's name in vain, using it casually or as a curse word? That's called blasphemy, and it's a violation of the Third Commandment. These are just half of the Ten Commandments. Have you broken even one in your whole life? The Bible gives us God's standard for keeping His Law: "Whoever keeps the whole law and yet stumbles in one point, he has become guilty of all" (James 2:10).

Each and every one of us has sinned and broken God's Moral Law. We have all violated His holy commandments. The Bible says that "each one of us will give an account of himself to God" (Romans 14:12).

We will all have our day in court. God's Law is perfect. God's judgment is perfect. You and I are incapable of living up to God's perfect standard and, like the young man in custody, you need to realize that when your day in court comes you will be found guilty of violating God's Law. The sentence? "The wages of sin is death" (Romans 6:23). The punishment is the torment of hell for all eternity. Given that, please carefully consider the following.

Attorney for the Defense

If you put your trust and hope in your ability to argue, explain, or justify the reasons for the sin in your life; if you're counting on a benevolent god—a god you've created in your own mind (which is idolatry), who will simply turn a blind eye and will exonerate you of your sin, you will be disappointed. You will be like the accused criminal who arrogantly goes into court and insists on defending himself. You will have your day in court, and you will lose your case.

But there is hope. God has provided the perfect Attorney—One who has never lost a case. Writing to Christians in the first century, the apostle John states: "If anyone sins, we have an Advocate with the Father, Jesus Christ the righteous; and He Himself is the propitiation [payment] for our sins; and not for ours only, but also for those of the whole world" (1 John 2:1,2). The apostle Paul explains: "There is one God, and one mediator also between God and men, the man Christ Jesus, who gave Himself as a ransom for all" (1 Timothy 2:5).

One day you will find yourself seated at the eternal defense table, accused of sinning against God. Think about it. How would you feel if you were arrested for residential burglary and you arrive in court, only to find out that the house you broke into belongs to the judge?

If you sit at the defense table alone, you will be found guilty as charged. As such, you will be sentenced to eternity in hell. But, if you turn from your sins (repent) and put your faith in Jesus Christ as your Lord and Savior, He will be your Advocate. He lived a sinless life, died on the cross for your sins, and was raised from the dead. He is your only hope of an acquittal. Jesus Christ paid the full penalty for your sins—past, present, and future. Justice was served, the fine was paid, and the Judge can now set you free. Through this perfect act of love, God, the righteous and holy Judge, provided your only way of escape from the wrath and judgment to come.

> God so loved the world, that He gave His only begotten Son, that whoever believes in Him shall not perish, but have eternal life. For God did not send the Son into the world to judge the world, but that the world should be saved through Him. He who believes in Him is not judged; he who does not believe has been judged already, because he has not believed in the name of the only begotten Son of God. (John 3:16–18)

If you do not already know Jesus Christ as your Lord and Savior, my hope is that you will turn from your sins and place your trust in Him, for salvation is given only by the grace of God, through faith in Jesus Christ. My prayer is that you will do that today, so that you can one day walk out of the eternal courtroom, not as a convicted sinner bound for hell, but as a forgiven child of God bound for heaven. Then you will know the reality that Paul speaks of:

> There is therefore now no condemnation to those who are in Christ Jesus. (Romans 8:1)

If you recognize that you are guilty of breaking God's Law and want to be forgiven, then you must repent of (turn from) your sins and ask God to forgive you. There is nothing magical about the words you say. It is the condition of your heart before God that matters. You can pray something like this:

> Heavenly Father, I know that I am a sinner. I know that I can do nothing to earn Your forgiveness and salvation that You freely give. I believe that Jesus Christ is the Savior and that He is the only way to heaven. I believe He died on the cross to pay for my sins, and rose again so that my sins can be forgiven. I ask You, Jesus, to be my Savior and the Lord of my life. Amen.

If you've prayed a prayer like this, genuinely repented of your sins, and given control of your life over to Jesus Christ as your Lord, you can trust the Scriptures that say salvation is real and cannot be taken away from you. This doesn't give us license to live any way we want to. A person who comes to a genuine faith in Christ will not live a perfect life, but a life in which the desire of the heart is to please God and live according to His will.

When you "put on the Lord Jesus Christ" (Romans 13:14) by giving your life to Him, He will clothe you with His spiritual armor. He is faithful. He will equip you to stand firm in your faith until the day you go to spend eternity with Him in heaven. Clothed with the armor of God, you can be victorious in every spiritual battle you face!

If you have placed your faith in Jesus Christ as your Lord and Savior, I would love to hear about it and welcome you into the body of Christ. Please send your *Take Up The Shield* testimonies to:

info@takeuptheshield.com

Ten-Four Ministries is available to help you grow in your faith. Feel free to contact us:

Ten-Four Ministries
P.O. Box 52005
Tulsa, OK 74152-9998
www.TenFourMinistries.org

For additional information about Ten-Four Ministries, or to help share this book with law enforcement officers, please see the following page.

TAKE UP THE SHIELD PROJECT

The goal of this project is to distribute copies of *Take Up the Shield* to members of the first responder community and military personnel in the U.S. and around the world. This is accomplished by providing bulk quantities of the book, at a significant discount, to churches, organizations, and individuals who agree to distribute the book to officers, firefighters, and/or soldiers free of charge.

Since its inception, the Take Up The Shield Project has placed the book (and thus the gospel) into the hands of thousands of brave public servants across the U.S., Canada, Australia, Europe, and Africa.

For more information about how you can participate, visit www.TakeUpTheShield.com.

TEN-FOUR MINISTRIES

Ten-Four Ministries also provides the following practical and spiritual support to the law enforcement community:

The Armor of God Project: Through donations of used, but fully functional vests, this effort provides protective body armor to officers who cannot afford their own, in the U.S. and around the world.

Uniform Cross Ministry: This aspect of the ministry provides free cross pins for the uniforms of first responders. Contact us at cross@tenfourministries.org.

Missions: Ten-Four Ministries is committed to the proclamation of Jesus Christ as Lord and part of that effort is coordinated trips across the world. In providing training to other agencies or responding to disaster zones, we proclaim Christ as King. Find out more at www.warriormissions.org.

NOTES

1. Peter T. O'Brien, *The Pillar New Testament Commentary—The Letter to the Ephesians* (Grand Rapids, MI: Eerdmans Publishing, 1999), p. 465.

2. Martyn Lloyd-Jones, *The Sovereign Spirit* (Wheaton, IL: Harold Shaw Publishers, 1985), p. 58.

3. Officer Down Memorial Page <www.odmp.org/officer/17545-police-officer-james-mitchell-mitch-prince>.

4. O'Brien, *The Pillar New Testament Commentary*, p. 472.

5. John MacArthur, *The MacArthur New Testament Commentary—Ephesians* (Chicago: Moody Press, 1986), p. 351.

6. "A History of Body Armor—Bullet Proof Vests" <www.inventors.about.com/library/inventors/blforensic3.htm>.

7. MacArthur, *The MacArthur New Testament Commentary*, p. 352.

8. "Slain Officer Wore No Bulletproof Vest, Supervisor Says," Dec. 8, 2003 <www.policeone.com/news/73777-Slain-Officer-Wore-No-Bulletproof-Vest-Supervisor-Says>.

9. "Boston Special Ops Cop Survives Shooting; Saved by Protective Vest," Laurel J. Sweet, David Weber, and Kevin Rothstein, *Boston Herald*, Feb. 11, 2004 <www.policeone.com/police-products/tactical/body-armor/articles/79021>.

10. R. Kent Hughes, *Ephesians—The Mystery of the Body of Christ* (Wheaton, IL: Crossway Books, 1990), p. 232.

11. William Hendriksen, *New Testament Commentary—Ephesians* (Grand Rapids, MI: Baker Books, 1967), p. 277.

12. Hughes, *Ephesians—The Mystery of the Body of Christ*, p. 233.

13. Ibid., p. 234.

14. MacArthur, *The MacArthur New Testament Commentary*, p. 358.

15. James Montgomery Boice, *An Expositional Commentary—Ephesians* (Grand Rapids, MI: Baker Books, 1997), p. 248.

16. Hughes, *Ephesians—The Mystery of the Body of Christ*, pp. 240–41.

17. Spurgeon, *Spiritual Warfare in a Believer's Life*, pp. 129–132.

18. MacArthur, *The MacArthur New Testament Commentary*, p. 368.

19. Boice, *An Expositional Commentary—Ephesians*, p. 253.

20. Hughes, *Ephesians—The Mystery of the Body of Christ*, p. 244.

21. B. B. Warfield, "The Inspiration of the Bible," a lecture. From Bibliotheca Sacra, vol. 51 (Oberlin, OH: Bibliotheca Sacra Company, 1894), p. 617. <www.biblicalstudies.org.uk/pdf/bsac/1894_614_warfield.pdf>.

22. I'm grateful to Ray Comfort for this illustration, as well as for teaching me the use of the Law in evangelism. Visit his website at www.livingwaters.com.